D1075145

The
Making
of a
Therapist

A PRACTICAL GUIDE FOR THE INNER JOURNEY

Louis Cozolino

W. W. NORTON & COMPANY
New York · London

For information about permission to reproduce
selections from this book, write to
Permissions, W. W. Norton & Company, Inc.,
500 Fifth Avenue, New York, NY 10110

Production Manager: Leann Graham
Manufacturing by Quebecor World Fairfield

Library of Congress Cataloging-in-Publication Data

Cozolino, Louis J.
The making of a therapist : a practical guide for the inner
journey / Louis J. Cozolino.
    p.   cm.
  "A Norton professional book"—P.
  Includes bibliographical references.
  ISBN 0-393-70424-6
  1. Psychotherapy—Vocational guidance.
2. Psychotherapists—Psychology. 3. Psychotherapist
and patient. I. Title.
RC440.8.C696 2004
616.89'14'023—dc22   2004043392

W. W. Norton & Company, Inc., 500 Fifth Avenue,
New York, NY 10110
www.wwnorton.com

W. W. Norton & Company Ltd., Castle House,
75/76 Wells St., London W1T 3QT

5 7 9 0 8 6 4

*This book is lovingly dedicated
to the Lieberman family,
Bonnie, Ileene, Sheila, and Marvin,
and to the memory of
Ethel Baumohl.*

Contents

Acknowledgments

I WOULD LIKE TO THANK my editor at Norton Professional Books, Deborah Malmud, for her support, guidance, and encouragement through the conceptualization and writing of this book. Many thanks also go to Bruce Singer and Sharon Grambo for their invaluable editorial and creative input.

I am deeply indebted to David Gorton, Faith McClure, and John Wynn, friends and colleagues who enthusiastically contributed their considerable knowledge and wisdom to this endeavor. Thanks also to Hans Miller, Allan Schore, and Dan Siegel for their ongoing moral support and creative input. Finally, I want to thank Susan for always knowing how to make me smile.

Introduction

Never, never, for the sake of peace, deny
your own experience.
—DAG HAMMARSKOLD

I WAS ABOUT TO START my first session as a therapist and about to have my first panic attack. All I could do was lean against the clinic wall and feel my body flush with perspiration. After years of sitting in classrooms, I couldn't remember a thing I had learned. Forget about that— I couldn't even remember my client's name. Was it Janice? JoAnne? Joanie? I stared at the clock on the wall, my head spinning faster than the second hand racing toward the hour.

"Are you ready?" It was my supervisor's voice. I looked at him like a scared 5-year-old and he seemed to understand. He placed a calming hand on my shoulder and his expression reassured me that it was normal to be scared. "Just remember five things and you'll be fine." This is what he told me:

- No matter what happens, don't panic;
- The client is more nervous than you are;

- If you don't know what's happening, keep quiet until you do;
- The client will assume you know what you're doing; and, most importantly,
- *Just make it through the hour!*

Armed with this wisdom, I ventured toward the waiting room to meet my client, all the while repeating under my breath, "Just make it through the hour, just make it through the hour!"

I didn't say much during that first session. My client was a very dramatic aspiring actress. When she wasn't striding back and forth across the room, she was curled up on the couch. She poured out her heart about her family, her lovers, and her stalled career. Meanwhile, I sat, listened, tried to keep calm, and nodded knowingly like the therapists I had seen on training videos. Somehow, I remembered to ask the necessary questions, communicate my concern, and, yes, even call her by the right name.

Soon the hour was up. As she walked out the door she said she felt better and would be back next week. I stood and watched her turn the corner before I let out a sigh of relief; I had made it through my first session! As the months went by, I settled into my new role as a therapist. Gradually, I shifted from "survival mode" to one of being able to stay calm, listen, and try to be helpful. My early sessions had served their purpose: I was becoming acclimated to sitting across from a client.

Imagination and Reality

Each of us is an experiment of nature, a unique combination of biology and experience giving rise to our strengths, frailties, and hopes. Although we are only human, many of us strive to be more than human. We are blessed with minds capable of constructing ideal images of whom we hope to be and burdened by our disappointments in not living up to these unrealistic standards. The beginning of a new career is a time when imagination and reality collide, when our fantasies are put to the test in the light of day and in the presence of witnesses. If you are reading this book, you have likely arrived at such a point in your life. When you train to be a therapist, you discover that it is not just your intellect that gets tested, but also your judgment, empathy, and maturity. Becoming a psychotherapist is indeed a challenge to both heart and soul.

Like most other professional careers, being a psychotherapist involves mastering a large and ever-growing body of knowledge, learning a variety of skills, and navigating complex relationships. Unlike with other professions, being a competent therapist requires a simultaneous exploration of one's inner world and private thoughts. When we begin training, we embark on two simultaneous journeys: one outward into the professional world and the other inward, through the labyrinths of our own psyches.

The complexity of this inner journey is inadequately addressed in most classes and books for beginners. In this book I cover some familiar topics (such as making interpretations, cultural sensitivity, and identifying resistance), but my true focus is on the *personal* and *emotional* aspects of these issues, as they affect the therapist. In the following chapters, I hope to provide you with a new way of thinking about your experience of being a therapist—one that involves shuttling between a focus on the client and an attention to your own internal experience both inside and outside of the therapy session. The best therapeutic work occurs when these two streams of awareness are interwoven within the therapist.

Over the years, I have had many students who desired to become therapists while sealing off their inner worlds. They tried to stay "above the neck" in the hope of avoiding their own feelings and emotions. I often felt sadness when interacting with these trainees because I could sense the pain beneath their need for disconnection. Unfortunately, this intellectualizing defense handicaps both personal growth and the development of good therapeutic abilities. For most students of psychotherapy, the primary challenge is not mastering the academic material, it is summoning the emotional courage to move through the inner space that leads to knowing oneself. The more fearless we become in the exploration of our inner worlds, the greater our self-knowledge and our ability to help our clients.

Discovering and Taming the Unconscious

A few years ago, I took a trip to visit my friend Jason and his son Joey. Three-year-old Joey was an extremely social, observant, and energetic little guy. He would get up early each morning, come into the guest room where I was sleeping, and climb into bed beside me. I would pretend I was asleep as long as I could, hoping to preserve those last few minutes before starting the day. But my playing possum tested Joey's patience; he began singing songs into my ear.

When that didn't work, he developed a strategy of baiting me with questions such as, "Uncle Lou, what's your favorite game?" or "Uncle Lou, do you want French toast for breakfast?" One morning, Joey was unusually still. Eventually, I felt him gently patting and stroking my hair. Finally, he said quietly, "Uncle Lou, what's wrong with your hair?" This time, I took the bait. "What's *wrong* with my hair?" He replied in his most earnest 3-year-old voice, "It's too soft for real hair." I had to smile. You see, Joey is African-American and I'm not.

Like Joey, we all see the world from our own perspective and through the prism of our unconscious assumptions. How else can it be? Egocentrism comes naturally to us because of the way our brains process information, yet none of us feels that our perspective contains biases. The way we see things simply seems correct. The problem with this belief is that our vision of reality and sense of conscious control are mere illusions.

We are guided and directed by multiple unconscious processes of memory and emotion. It is not a character flaw but a biological "given" that we have to accept. Our temperaments and personal histories create patterns of thinking and feeling that direct our behavior outside of our awareness. Although we all begin life in a state of complete egocentrism, we can learn to have a broader perspective through experience and education. Learning about our personal, cultural, and human biases should be a primary focus of the training of every therapist.

Regardless of theoretical orientation, all true psychotherapeutic interventions are interpersonal, delivered by one human being to another. There is no generic therapist or average client, only relationships between two or more people with personalities, predilections, and prejudices. Despite the growing influence of hard science on our field, psychotherapy remains a human and imperfect art.

A therapist, unlike an accountant or engineer, does not

have the choice to do his work disconnected from personal experience and deep emotions. The private personal world of the therapist is, in fact, one of our most important tools. What we don't know about ourselves won't just hurt us, it will negatively affect the therapeutic relationship. We can maximize the unique healing potential that we bring to each client only when we see and understand our personal past.

Despite its central importance to the psychotherapeutic process, a focus on self-knowledge has faded from training as brief therapy and psychopharmacology have taken center stage. A psychiatric resident whom I supervised asked me how many hours of therapy I had done before graduating from my doctoral program. After some mental arithmetic, I came up with approximately 6,000. He calculated that by the time he graduated from his residency, he would have only 50. He asked, "How can I be ready to do therapy after 50 hours of training?" I said, "I have no idea." After 6,000 supervised hours, I had still felt like a beginner.

It is difficult and costly to train therapists properly. It is far easier to provide a series of classes and leave the personal, more difficult components of therapeutic training to others. The therapist's personal growth, a focus that was once woven together with academic learning, has been marginalized or ignored to the detriment of both therapists in training and the clients who will one day go to them for treatment.

As therapists, our greatest challenges arise from our personal conflicts and the shared limitations of being human. Throughout this book, I refer to these conflicts and limitations we bring to our work under the broad term of *countertransference*. Countertransference is distortion of the therapy relationship that occurs because of the therapist's unconscious. The therapist's countertransference can usually be traced to common human struggles with shame, attachment, and fear of abandonment. The power of these primal experiences causes us to unconsciously mix up our own emotional struggles with those of our clients. Attempting to tame the unconscious influences on our experience of our clients is a formidable challenge we all face.

Have you ever been to a circus and seen lions and lion tamers? How do those tamers step into the cage night after night? They succeed because they have a set of principles, techniques, and skills that allow them to develop a working relationship with their beasts. For example, the lion tamer enters the cage before the lion in order to establish territorial dominance. The cage is round, leaving no place for the lion to hide or escape. It is always made clear to the lion that the food it receives comes from the beneficence of the tamer. The lion tamer usually works with the less dominant lion in the pride, who is more likely to be motivated to establish an alliance with the trainer against the more dominant lions. These principles, based on the workings of the lions' brains and the rules of their social order, allow the tamer to develop a working relationship with a far more powerful animal.

The unconscious mind is like a wild lion. We can never overpower our unconscious, only learn about it and hope to gain its cooperation. Taming the unconscious requires getting to know it well enough to develop a healthy working relationship. Sometimes it will get out of control and require more work and training. And, lest we forget, from time to time, lion tamers do get attacked! There are strategies, techniques, and safeguards to make the unconscious more manageable and cooperative—more helpful and less dangerous to yourself and your clients. I will discuss these taming techniques and strategies throughout this book.

The Goals of this Book

A basic goal of this book is to give beginning therapists permission to feel what they inevitably will feel—uncertainty, confusion, and fear—while also offering some strategies and advice for dealing with common situations that all therapists face. Accepting these feelings (and then using them to our advantage) is a powerful and often overlooked aspect of psychotherapeutic training.

In the chapters ahead, I will explore the experience of becoming a therapist by shuttling back and forth between the *objective* aspects of therapy and the *personal* experience of becoming (and being) a therapist. I have chosen this method of shuttling between inner and outer worlds to serve as a model for the actual experience of doing therapy. Shuttling requires that we remain flexible in order to move between our minds and bodies, thoughts and feelings, and between ourselves and our clients. The subjective experience of psychotherapy is ultimately the result of the ebb and flow of conscious energy between two or more human beings.

The focus, then, is biased in the direction of feeling rather than thinking, of human interactions rather than the content of what is said, and, most importantly, is based on you, the therapist. My hope is that you will use your training to serve your own personal growth as you learn your new profession. I encourage you to seek out trusted teachers and well-trained therapists to assist you.

Although it is embarrassing to admit, I expected to be a great therapist from my very first session. I had extreme difficulty giving myself the time and understanding to make mistakes and gradually improve; I felt that I needed to be competent from the very beginning. I have since learned that becoming a competent therapist takes many years; being a great therapist takes a lifetime. I hereby give you permission to start off not knowing a single thing about how to do psychotherapy. Try to relax, remember to breathe, and take the time to learn. If nothing else, just make it through the book!

Let us now embark on the inner journey.

THE MAKING OF A THERAPIST

PART ONE

Getting Through Your First Sessions

CHAPTER ONE

What Have I Gotten Myself Into?

> Only as a warrior can one survive the path
> of knowledge.
>> —DON JUAN

SO YOU'VE STARTED your training as a therapist and all you can think is, "I feel like a fraud." Or to put it more kindly, you may ask, "How can I do this when I am so confused and have so many problems of my own?" Countless times over the years I have been pulled aside by students and told some version of the following: "Here I am trying to help my clients, meanwhile I feel like I'm going nuts. How can I help someone else when I'm struggling with my own issues? I used to think that I was sane, but I'm not sure anymore. I should have listened to my father and been a lawyer. At least they don't have to be sane." Sound familiar? Because I've heard statements like this from so many students (and experienced them myself), I've come to see that these feelings may be a common hurdle on the path to becoming a therapist. We all need to become aware of our pain and uncertainties and then grow through them. What makes a good therapist is personal courage; the courage to face one's fears, limitations, and confusion.

Why are therapists so vulnerable to doubts about our competence and sanity? We are, by nature, prone to self-examination, and what therapist hasn't seen him- or herself reflected in the cases he or she studies? We have a sense of our own fears, insecurities, and "craziness" while we accord others their polished social presentation. Then there is the fact that we therapists tend to come from families in which emotional conflicts interfered with our getting the help and guidance we needed while growing up. Most therapists grew up struggling to be loved and accepted by others. Because of these early experiences, many of us find it difficult to believe others can be of help to us. We carry this struggle into our adult lives and, inevitably, into our relationships with our clients.

A mistake I made during my training was trying to impress my supervisors with how good a therapist I was. I would present my successes, downplay my failures, and hide my confusion. This defense, similar to the one I employed during childhood, only enhanced my sense of being a fraud. I was putting on a show and gaining approval, all the while undermining my confidence and training. A breakthrough in my training and personal growth came when I found the courage to appear weak, uncertain, and share my mistakes openly.

At what point are we healthy enough to help other people? It is normal for human beings to be confused, and all of us have problems and issues. Therapists are never "done" with growth, they are simply people who should be dedicated to learning as much about themselves and others as they possibly can. The best therapists are fully human and engage in the struggles of life. Our own failures help us to remain open to the struggles of others; our personal victories give us the optimism and courage to inspire those struggling with their lives.

Do we need to have our lives in order before we can help someone? If that were the case, few clients would ever get helped! Life is messy, and each new stage brings new challenges. Buddhists describe the self as an endlessly peeling onion, every discovery revealing new layers to explore and uncover. This has certainly been my experience as I am repeatedly awakened to new discoveries of my own ignorance. A good therapist is not perfect but simply a person dedicated to ongoing self-discovery and lifelong learning. We continue to live and grow with and through our limitations.

The key to ongoing growth, to continue to peel the onion, is transparency and openness to feedback. In other words, sharing what is going on inside and struggling to understand your therapists, supervisors, and trusted advisors. You can't do this alone.

"I Don't Know"

You never know who will end up being your teacher. Years ago, while wandering through a flea market, I encountered an elderly gentleman named Emmett. He caught my attention because of his wild white hair and the large button on his chest with the words "I Don't Know." My fascination with interesting characters led me to ask about his button and, as is often the case in such encounters, a long and detailed story ensued.

Apparently, his inquisitive young grandson had recently begun asking a new question every 20 seconds. Despite Emmett's advanced age and intelligence, he was confronted with the reality of how few of his grandson's questions he was able to answer. He really didn't know where the sky came from, why people are mean to each other, or why God took Grandma to heaven and left him alone. These were questions he had long ago learned not to ask. Emmett was honest about his ignorance and repeatedly told his grandson that he didn't know.

The child's frustration grew to the point where he finally shouted, "I don't know, I don't know! Grandpa, what *do* you know?" After a long career as an engineer and manager, answering hundreds of questions every day, Emmett was stumped by a 4-year-old. Emmett was a remarkable man. Unembarrassed by his ignorance, he made no attempt to cover it up. Instead of providing easy answers, he took responsibility for helping his grandson to discover his own answers. This attitude allowed him to explore ideas and feelings, look things up when that was possible, and openly discuss complicated and emotionally difficult questions. Emmett said that he felt he learned as much as his grandson during their discussions and wore the button to remind him that ignorance is the door to new learning.

Awakening to ignorance has been a persistent theme in wisdom philosophy everywhere in the world throughout time. When the oracle at Delphi told Socrates that he was the wisest of men, Socrates assumed that the oracle was mistaken; he was certain of his own ignorance. It later dawned on him, while watching the folly of those convinced of their knowledge, that the oracle recognized his awareness of his ignorance as wisdom. This same insight is a core teaching of the many schools of Buddhism that focus on seeing past the illusions of the mind and the material world. If you recognize and accept your ignorance, you will not only be a better therapist, you will also be in the good company of Buddha, Socrates, and my new friend Emmett.

Giving Yourself Permission To Not Know

Give yourself permission to not know. Like Emmett, nurture relationships with your clients that include your limitations and allow for honest exploration. Be supportive of yourself, be reasonable in demands on your progress, and reinforce your strengths and what you *are* able to accomplish. Instead of comparing yourself to teachers or master clinicians you see on tape, use an internal yardstick to judge your progress: Compare where *you* are now to where *you* were 6 months ago. In psychotherapy, there is infinite room for improvement and, in turn, infinite room for self-criticism. Your ignorance is not a bottomless pit, it is a container to be filled with knowledge and experience.

Jeff was a new therapist working with an irritable client we came to call "the angry guy." Each session, the angry guy demanded that Jeff provide him with simple solutions to complex problems. He would come in with a list of questions such as "How do I find a girlfriend?" and "What career should I pursue?" only to be disappointed when the session ended without an answer. He would stand, look Jeff in the eye, and say, "What kind of therapist are you?" then shake his head with profound disapproval and walk out of the office.

This took its toll on Jeff and he began to feel bad about his therapeutic abilities. He would try to offer some practical advice to the angry guy, but was always told that he should "return to the drawing board." Jeff felt frustrated and increasingly angry with the angry guy. It seemed Jeff could do nothing right. I told him, "It's not about you knowing what your client should do, it's about you providing a relationship in which he can discover himself." I suggested that instead of coming up with answers, he try to share how his client made him feel.

Jeff's expression told me that he thought my suggestion was a bit wacky but he was willing to give it a try. During the next session, Jeff shared his own feelings of sadness, frustration, and anger with trying so hard to be helpful only to be shot down again and again. The angry guy listened intently, arms crossed over his chest, his expression growing more and more stern. Finally, he burst out, "Now you know how *I* feel." The angry guy went on to tell Jeff about his relationship with his parents, their constant dissatisfaction, and his ongoing sense of shame about being a failure as a son. This was the first time he had discussed his family or his past with Jeff, and it was the beginning of a fruitful stage of therapy.

In order for this kind of interaction to take place, Jeff had to take himself out of the position of expert. Instead, he had to be a thinking, feeling, and available human being willing to share his experiences with his client. He had to admit to himself and his client that he didn't know the answer to his client's questions. What Jeff had to offer was a willingness to stay connected through the process of exploring his client's inner world. The angry guy was demonstrating his childhood to Jeff through their relationship.

Many of us harbor the fantasy that we will walk into a therapy session, save the client from suffering, and take the therapeutic world by storm. Jeff received a loud wake-up call from the angry guy that this fantasy is utterly unrealistic. Therapy stalled until Jeff accepted the stance of not knowing.

Following are some things to check in order to make sure you are retaining a stance of not knowing:

- Do you feel certain that what you are doing is the right thing?
- Do you continue to bring a client back to an interpretation again and again, even if he or she continues to reject it?
- Do you feel passionate about the truth of your form of psychotherapy?
- Do you find yourself dismissing your supervisor's ideas if they differ from your own?
- Do you feel like a failure if you don't have an acceptable answer for a client's question?

If you answered yes to any of these questions, it is time to reexamine your feelings, motivations, and assumptions about being a therapist. Don't be afraid to look at these issues; exploring them can only lead you to greater self-understanding. My insecurity and fear of looking stupid made learning much more difficult than it had to be. I missed many opportunities to learn because I was unable to say I didn't know.

Desperately Seeking Systems

If you are anything like I am, your first instinct will be to become a disciple of some charismatic leader or particular system of psychotherapy. Freud. Ellis. Bowen. Beck. These "superstars" of psychology, each with his own theory, tempt the novice therapist to follow slavishly in his path. I so badly wanted something true to hold onto in the midst of my early confusion that I bounced from one guru to another, desperately seeking a system to believe in.

Although systems make us feel more confident and powerful, they can also limit what we learn and what we are able to see. Throughout my training I have been impressed by both the positive results each mode of therapy is capable of achieving and what vital aspects of a person each seems to ignore. Let me give you an example.

A couple of years into my training, there was an earthquake during a session. Not a huge one, but strong enough to make the entire room sway for 5 or 10 seconds. True to my analytic training, I sat quietly and watched my client's eyes grow wider as the room came alive. My stoicism only seemed to confuse him. "I think it's an earthquake!" he finally said. Without moving, I softly responded, "Yes. How do you feel about that?" The thought of this strange interaction always makes me laugh at myself. How could it have resulted in anything other than making my client think *I* was crazy? Or even worse, that *he* was crazy for having a normal reaction to a frightening situation. My adherence to a system made me feel like I knew what I was doing at the cost of having an authentic connection with my client.

Given the complexity of our human behaviors, emotions, and relationships, confusion and uncertainty are inevitable. Because uncertainty makes us so anxious, we look for quick, clear, and definitive answers. Graduate students, in particular, can easily get caught in the spell of a teachers' biases and the certainty they portray. Try to keep an open mind despite the attempts of others to close it. Work with the best people you can find regardless of orientation, and, most importantly, get training in a variety of perspectives. Knowledge of a variety of perspectives is the best defense against false certainty.

Our discomfort with uncertainty, particularly when we are new to a profession and without a wealth of our own experience to draw on, pushes us toward premature closure on questions of diagnosis, interpretations, and treatment strategy. Research has shown that given an hour to diagnose a client, mental health practitioners tend to decide on a diagnosis in the first few minutes and then selectively gather data supportive of their initial hypothesis. Latching onto a quick diagnosis is on par with becoming a zealous devotee of a therapy guru. Let's face it, the more insecure we are, the more vulnerable we will be to "conversion" experiences to new therapeutic modalities. Ask yourself this question: Is my devotion to a theory or technique reflective of my own personal struggles, or is it a rationally chosen theoretical orientation that is actually helpful for the person sitting across from me?

It can take courage to choose a course of action and pursue it. It also takes courage to admit a mistake and take a different approach. Think of the parable of the difference between a rat and a human being. If you move the cheese from where a rat expects it to be, it will eventually look somewhere else. A human being, on the other hand, will look for the cheese in the same place forever. Why? Because we humans "believe" the cheese *should* be there! Our beliefs guide our behavior, but our beliefs are often wrong. Simple answers, although emotionally satisfying, can often be quite limited, especially when we are dealing with creatures as complex as human beings.

Dreams of the Messiah

When a client first walks into your office, you never know whether or not you will be able to be of help. Some clients may just be a bad match with you and, with luck, they will move on to another therapist who can help them. Many clients see a number of therapists over the years, each of whom plays a role in their growth and healing. I have seen clients who ended up doing the bulk of their most successful work with other therapists, whereas others have thanked me for helping them when no one else could. What feels like unsuccessful therapy may be the groundwork for a later relationship that will be very successful. Although this once frustrated me, I now imagine that while I'm preparing someone for some future therapeutic success somewhere else, another therapist is doing the groundwork with a future client of mine.

Not too long after I began my training I had an embarrassing and enlightening dream. In my dream, I was sitting across from a client who was a composite of four or five of my clients. That their facial features, gestures, and problems merged into a single client made some kind of dream sense. I sat, not really listening, but rather thinking about what to say next. Preparing to speak, I felt a rush of emotion as if I were about to say something profound. A chorus of angels began to sing. Beams of sunlight penetrated the ceiling. I half expected God to walk through the door—until I realized that *I* was playing His role.

I sat up in bed, surprised, laughing a bit, but suddenly very clear. My fantasy of my role as a therapist was connected to salvation. I realized that I saw my job as saving my clients by saying or doing something miraculous. Although it took many months in my own therapy to explore the origins and implications of this dream, the immediate message was painfully obvious: I was setting myself up for failure. How can a mere mortal live up to the biblical achievements my unconscious had absorbed from Hollywood extravaganzas?

We all come to training with some unconscious mission to fulfill: to find ourselves, preserve our sanity, or save someone in our family. Many of us grow up being told what good listeners we are, how well we negotiate family conflict, or how we manage to regulate the emotions of those around us. Whatever it is, we can be better therapists when these missions are identified, understood, and factored into how we experience our clients. We are bound to fail with many of our clients if we operate primarily from unconscious fantasies. When the waters don't part, when the grand fantasies go bust, we become vulnerable to our own depression and despair and risk turning our careers into drudgery.

To accept our clients, we have to first learn to accept ourselves. This can be the biggest challenge of all.

CHAPTER TWO

Getting Centered
and
Learning to Listen

Anybody can get worked up if they have
the intention. It's peacefulness that is hard
to come by . . . .
—BARBARA KINGSOLVER

AT THE HEART OF our work as therapists is our
ability to get centered, stay focused, and listen. For this we
need to access all of our intellectual and emotional capabilities. Thinking and feeling are both vital to staying centered
and gently guiding the direction of therapy.

Your relationship with a client begins the moment you
receive the initial call to set up an appointment. Your openness, curiosity, and concern are conveyed through focused
attention and tone of voice. Remember, you don't get a second chance to make a first impression! Evolution has primed
our brains to size someone up as fast as possible, so first
impressions have a significant and sustained impact on how
others experience us.

Try to return the first (and all) phone calls to your clients in the same state of mind that you do psychotherapy. Don't call them while you are watching television, having a fight with your spouse, or driving in traffic. Whenever possible, call clients from a land-based phone so their experience of you isn't contaminated with static and lost connections. Be mindful of the fact that all of a client's interactions with you are a part of their experience of therapy. Billing questions, appointment changes, and calls for comfort are all aspects of the relationship and possess therapeutic value.

Don't be under the impression that you are starting with a blank slate. Although your work with a client begins with the first phone call, your client's relationship with you begins long before the first contact. It rests in their past experience with caretakers, doctors, and other therapists. These past experiences are intermingled with their hopes and fears about what will happen once they enter the consulting room. Each new client has a history of positive and negative expectations that will emerge in the course of the therapeutic relationship.

Begin by being openly curious about your client's thoughts and expectations about therapy. Consider asking questions like:

- Have you been in therapy before?
- What was it like for you?
- What do you think of therapy and therapists?
- Do you know other people who have been helped or hurt by therapy?
- What do you hope to get from our time together?

Try to avoid becoming defensive when clients attack past therapists or express doubts about *your* skills and abilities.

These memories, feelings, and concerns are all part of the therapeutic relationship and potentially contain important information about your new client. If you *do* find yourself being defensive, take a deep breath and reflect on your feelings. What buttons is your client pressing? Is he or she really attacking you or is it your own insecurity and vulnerability that make you feel that way? These are excellent issues to explore with your supervisors and personal therapist. Our clients need us to be strong and centered enough to withstand criticism and attacks that we may not deserve. These attacks are often forms of memory that our clients need help to become aware of and understand.

Take Time to Get Centered

Clients are very sensitive to the emotional and interpersonal background of therapy. I treasured the tranquility of my own therapist's office and those sessions became the centerpoint of my week. Your therapeutic stance should contain a mixture of quiet calm and alert attentiveness. Many therapists I know are extremely overcommitted, distracted, and never fully focused on any client. Clients have commented to me about past therapists who seemed continually preoccupied, agitated, irritable, and, believe it or not, even took phone calls during sessions! This isn't because they were stupid or didn't care, they were just overwhelmed with the volume of what they had to keep track of each day. It will help both you and your clients to make the consulting room a safe haven from the chaos of daily life.

A frenetic therapist is not a good therapist. These five basic strategies will help you stay centered:

- Allow extra time to get to your office so you don't arrive anxious or tense.
- Think of the 5 minutes before each session as a time to relax and get centered.
- Schedule breaks during the day for rest, reading, or social contacts.
- Don't overbook your week—avoid emotional and physical exhaustion.
- Monitor your emotional and physical state and adjust your schedule when needed.

Pay special attention to your consulting room. Create an environment in which you feel comfortable and surround yourself with the kinds of things that remind you to be calm and mindful. Comfortable furniture, pillows, and soft lighting contribute to an atmosphere of reflection and contemplation. I have a painting of children playing quietly at the beach, old books, and antique furniture to communicate consistency, solidity, and caring to my clients. I keep candles in my office and a small stereo to help me relax between sessions. I'll take the time to relax by stretching, reading the newspaper, or calling a friend. My office is full of books on travel, wisdom philosophy, and science. I even have a special drawer for snacks, drinks, and candy to treat myself. Think of your attention to your work environment and centering activities as an investment in your own peace of mind that pays dividends to your clients.

The Power of Listening

Our society is almost entirely action oriented. We measure our worth based on what we've done, what we are doing, and what we plan to accomplish. We carry appointment books, digital organizers, beepers, and cell phones, and our heads are filled with the sounds of voices, music, and traffic. In the whirlwind of activity we call our lives, listening has been demoted to a passive "nonactivity." Ironically, while all this is going on, we all long to be listened to by a caring and attentive other.

When I eavesdrop on conversations, I am often struck by how little people pay attention to one another. What passes for conversation is often alternating monologues; each person uses the other to trigger their own thoughts and associations. Sometimes, it almost seems that the art of listening is in danger of extinction. I suspect that one of the reasons why psychotherapy has been so successful in modern urban society is that it provides for the fundamental human need to be listened to for at least a few minutes each week.

Attentive listening is a central therapeutic skill and a valuable gift we can give to others. Your presence and attention are powerful agents of cure. Be mindful of your own inner pressure to fill in silences and come up with rapid solutions. Experiment with patience. I've found that if I am patient, clients will often arrive at the very same conclusions I wanted to give them minutes before. I suspect that it is much better for our clients to discover their own insights and feel satisfaction and pride in these discoveries.

The most helpful listening occurs in the context of a positive interpersonal relationship that includes warmth, appreciation, and respect. This context provides a matrix in which we can articulate our thoughts and come to better understand our inner worlds. We often have to hear what we're saying to know what we're thinking. Your job is to be that person who listens, so your clients can learn to listen to themselves.

Do you have basic listening skills? Ask yourself some of the following questions:

- Are you able to tune out distractions?
- Do you avoid interrupting your clients?
- Do you communicate interest through your body language and facial expressions?
- Do you read between the lines and hear the emotions behind the words?

Pay attention to these listening skills during sessions and when listening to tape recordings of your work.

Even as a novice therapist, you have a distinct advantage over your clients: You aren't them. I mean this in a good way. Simply by seeing the world through different eyes, you provide them with a different view of their words, behaviors, and feelings. By virtue of your vantage point, personal history, and defenses, you offer the possibility of new and potentially helpful insights into their world. The presence of an attentive therapist provides an invaluable service. It is, in fact, an essential cornerstone of psychotherapy.

Eye Contact

Eye contact is a powerful form of communication. For primates such as ourselves, eye gaze is central to establishing attachment, sending threat signals, and reading what may be on the minds of others. We are born with reflexes to turn toward others and look into their eyes. This "jumpstarts" the bonding process, triggers our brains to develop, and remains with us throughout life. Using our eyes and the facial expressions surrounding them, we communicate everything from deep love to intense hate. A roll of the eyes can cause shame, an open gaze can trigger sexual excitement, a raised eyebrow communicates our skepticism. The central importance of eye contact and facial expressions to survival has led to the evolution of extensive neural networks dedicated to interpreting their nearly infinite formations.

Based on our learning histories and cultural backgrounds, eye contact can come to mean many things. The same look will be experienced quite differently by different clients. Whereas one might feel comforted by a steady gaze, another will lash out and demand that you not stare. These reactions are unconsciously interwoven with other aspects of transference. Think of the reaction to eye contact as a form of implicit memory reflecting something that is potentially important about past experiences of love, hate, or shame. It can also provide insight into your client's level of anxiety, ability to form connections, and self-identity.

As with every other tool in psychotherapy, your ability to use eye contact successfully depends on self-understanding and personal insight. First, you need to understand what eye contact evokes in you. Your reaction can be understood in the context of your own history, culture, and personality. Try some of these questions on yourself:

- How comfortable am I with being looked at?
- What feelings and images does it evoke?
- What do I imagine that the person who is looking at me is thinking?
- Do I look differently at different clients?

- Am I communicating any of my feelings to my clients by the way I am looking at them? Am I angry, impatient with, or attracted to them?

What do you actually look like from your client's perspective? Are you staring intensely without blinking (which can be scary)? Does your eye contact make you look spaced out, disinterested, or angry? Learn how people tend to react to you and factor this knowledge in when interacting with clients, especially with those who appear timid, anxious, or have had particularly difficult relationships.

Don't panic when a client has a strong negative reaction to your gaze. Clients may startle you with a strong attack when you are quietly attending to their words. Be curious, not defensive; something was evoked within them that you want to know about. Focus on exploring their experience of you in that moment. Ask about their thoughts, feelings, suspicions, and fears. Ask them what they think is on *your* mind. Ask them if they have any memories of previous experiences where these same feelings were evoked. By examining these elements of their experience, you may discover some unconscious assumptions about you and other significant people in their life. In other words, your clients' eyes can be a window to their early bonding and attachment relationships.

On a practical note, it is usually best not to have chairs directly facing each other. Placing chairs at a slight angle makes it easier for a client to disengage from eye contact. It is also a good idea to ask your client once or twice during the first few sessions how it feels to be in the consulting room with you. This encourages them to discuss their experience of the session and their reaction to you. It also teaches them that discussing the emotional background of your interactions is a desirable part of the therapeutic process. Be willing to consider modifying the situation and your behavior to make a client more comfortable during the initial phase of therapy. Some clients need seating to be slightly farther apart; others may need you to look away for some part of the time. Therapy works best if your client oscillates between low and moderate levels of arousal. If your gaze, proximity, or some other aspect of the therapy situation is activating too much anxiety, it may interfere with the progress of your work.

Overall, my experience has been that most clients want you to be looking at them most of the time. Although they may not want to maintain constant eye contact with you, they may want to check in at regular intervals to make sure you are paying attention. I have asked some clients if they would feel more comfortable if I looked away instead of at them. All but the most anxious say that they want me to be looking at them. Looking away makes most clients feel that you are disinterested, bored, or preoccupied. Our sustained and committed attention is an essential aspect of successful therapy.

Communication Styles in Psychotherapy

Television and radio therapists may have to talk in entertaining "sound bites" but you don't. Giving your client your attention is far more important than thinking of clever things to say. Try to avoid being distracted by "brilliant" ideas. I learned this early in my training from my first supervisor. He listened to me offering one complex interpretation after another to my client. Finally, he pulled me aside and asked, "Do you think that he understands what you are saying? Have you noticed the puzzled look on his face?"

I was trying far too hard to make him *think* his way out of his pain and confusion. This intellectualized approach was a projection of my own defenses onto my clients (one of my many manifestations of countertransference). I slowly learned that if I had to concentrate that hard to figure out what to say, I should forget about making an interpretation and work on getting centered, staying focused, and listening.

The things most people need to learn in therapy are related to attachment, abandonment, love, and fear. We are trying to access basic emotional processes that are organized in primitive and early-developing parts of the brain. The language of these emotions is also very basic; it is the language of childhood. The more complex the language and ideas you bring into therapy, the more likely you are to stimulate your clients' intellectualizing defenses. The rule of KISS (keep it simple, stupid) may have been developed for design engineers, but it works very well for us, too.

The real prizes in therapy are emotional experiences flavored with cognition. These lead to changes in the quality of a client's life. We try to help our clients talk less and say more. Your style should be to get quickly to the point and stop. The clarity, brevity, and accuracy of a statement, combined with the silence that follows, increases its impact. It also allows the client time to process comments and make his or her own associations to them.

Consider the difference in the following two ways of talking to a sad client. You could say:

"I can see that you aren't as happy today as you would like to be and I'm wondering if you would say that you are feeling blue, depressed, hopeless, or anything like that or have felt like that over the last few days or weeks?"

Or you could say.

"I'm sorry you're feeling sad today."

If you are hearing a client struggling with his relationship with his father you could say:

"Your relationship with your father is problematic. There is competition between the two of you and it always feels like he is grading your achievements. It's hard to know whether he cares for you or that you make him feel better about himself when he takes credit for your accomplishments."

Or you could say.

"You wish your father could just love and accept you."

In both of these examples, the brief and straightforward expressions of clear emotions are far more powerful. They don't distract the client with too many words to attend to and understand. By stating an emotion and then getting out of the way of your clients' experience, you allow them to remain centered in their own experience.

Our communication style embodies our intellectual and interpersonal strengths as well as our defenses and coping mechanisms. Although they may be perfectly fine for day-to-day socializing, certain aspects of our style may interfere with optimal therapy. Therapeutically unhelpful communication styles, such as an overly intellectual approach, constant interpretation, or diagnosing every move a client makes protect us from our own uncomfortable emotions but do little to help our clients.

One day in a class, I chose two students to engage in a brief therapy dyad. As it happened, the student assigned to be the "client" had been in a car accident earlier that day. She was shaken and frightened and hesitantly told of her experience of being sideswiped at an intersection. As if he were conducting a police investigation, the "therapist" asked her scores of questions about the angle of impact, the make and model of both cars, and the speeds they were traveling when they hit. These questions cut off the client's feelings, forcing her to take care of her interrogator's needs. The interaction was clearly therapist-centered.

In the class discussion that followed the dyad, the therapist's communication style became the focus of attention. After some initial defensiveness, he said he was able to reflect on his emotional reaction to the client's experience. He admitted that he became anxious when he first heard about her accident. He had been involved in a serious car accident a year earlier and still suffered from a fear of driving, nightmares, and physical pain.

Through discussion, the therapist was able to get to his fear of what her feelings had triggered in him. Collecting facts and focusing on details helped him to steer her away from feelings and stay in control. Although his detective work took care of *his* emotional needs, he provided the client with little support and no empathy. The client later reported that the interaction was reminiscent of the way her parents tried to distract her from her feelings by giving her chores, art projects, and food. The obvious countertransference and untherapeutic nature of the interaction provided a valuable lesson for everyone.

Another common but unhelpful communication style is to rush to judgment and label the problem. Having a label provides an avenue of escape from confusion and makes us feel momentarily competent. But a label is not a cure and is only useful if it leads to helpful interventions. The worst consequence of labeling is settling on certain ideas and excluding other possibilities. This phenomenon, all too common in psychotherapy, is what I refer to as "premature hardening of the categories."

The way we treat our clients reflects our own needs, coping styles, and defenses. We reflexively assume that others will benefit from our defenses and we graciously (and unconsciously) try to teach others to use our personal strategies. It is a far more difficult task to take the time necessary to get to know someone in order to discover what *they* might need. To really know someone else means being willing to go where they need to go regardless of how it makes us feel. Just as our defenses protect us from parts of our inner worlds, our communication style protects us from aspects of our clients that make us anxious. As we learn more about our inner worlds, our communication styles expand, becoming more flexible and adaptable to the needs of others.

CHAPTER THREE

Now What
Do I Do?

> I know of no more encouraging fact than
> the unquestionable ability of man to ele-
> vate his life by a conscious endeavor.
> —HENRY DAVID THOREAU

THERAPY IS A WHIRLPOOL of words and thoughts, feelings and needs, difficult realities and fantasies. In the midst of so much complexity, beginning therapists struggle to maintain their bearings and sense of direction. Insecure and inexperienced in applying clinical theory to actual practice, they rely on gut instincts to guide them. In the absence of clinical experience, where do these instincts come from? For the most part, they are the product of our personal relationships, some of which will aid in therapy and some of which will not. In time we learn to sort them out. Instinct is a necessary but insufficient navigational tool to guide psychotherapy. Centeredness dissolves when we feel lost, and, without a case conceptualization and treatment plan, confusion will reign.

When I first started my training, I thought I had a foolproof method of helping my clients: I would convince them to handle their problems the way I handled my own. This meant not thinking about what was wrong, focusing on what they could do, and getting out there to work on things. When this brilliant approach failed—which was right away—I fumbled around with no real idea of what to do next. After faking it for a while, and feeling frustrated and embarrassed, I finally admitted to my supervisor that I was lost. Fortunately, he responded by saying, "Okay, let's get down to work." My first challenge was letting go of the belief that my own defenses and strategies would work for everyone. The second was applying psychological theory to my clinical work.

I soon discovered that applying what I had learned in the classroom to my work with clients took an entirely different set of skills than being a good student. The emotions of therapy, the complexity of a client's experience, and the sheer amount of information to process make applying theory in clinical situations difficult. Because of these challenges, having a clear and concise way of thinking about therapy (in general) and your client (in particular) is extremely helpful.

Although hundreds of methods of psychotherapy have been developed over the last century, only a few have survived the test of time. Currently, most psychotherapists use theories and techniques that fall into one of four general orientations: family systems, cognitive behavioral, psychodynamic, and client-centered or existential-humanistic. Some combination of these theories is at the heart of most forms of psychotherapy. Although a detailed discussion of each orientation is beyond the scope of this book, the following general principles can serve as a road map to help you stay on course.

Psychotherapy in a Nutshell

All orientations to therapy are designed to lessen suffering, reduce symptoms, and increase a client's ability to cope with the stressors of life. In the process of successful therapy we learn to experience, understand, and regulate emotion. Finally, each form of therapy teaches some new way of thinking about the self, others, and the world. In this part of the learning process, a new story of the self is formed through the interactions of client and therapist.

At its most basic level, psychotherapy is an interpersonal learning environment similar in many ways to proper parenting. In both, we tend to learn best when supported by a nurturing relationship with an empathic other, while being encouraged to confront life's challenges. We also learn best in a moderate state of arousal; too little puts us to sleep and too much triggers a fight-flight state that makes positive learning impossible.

Each form of psychotherapy strives to create a personal experience designed to:

- Examine assumptions and beliefs
- Expand awareness
- Increase reality testing
- Aid in confronting anxiety-provoking experiences
- Modify negative self-talk
- Develop a new and more adaptive life narrative

Therapy explores and examines behaviors, emotions, sensations, and cognitions with the goal of expanded awareness and increased integration of these realms of human experience. In most cases, the primary focus of psychotherapy is the integration of affect and cognition (feelings and thoughts). Through the alternating activation of emotional and cognitive processes, the brain is able to interconnect neural networks responsible for these two functions. The various schools of therapy differ primarily in the emphasis they place on each of the human functions and the techniques they employ to regulate and integrate them. Depending on your theoretical orientation, the result of this process is called *ego-strength, affect regulation, differentiation,* or *symptom reduction.*

What to Say, What to Do

The question about what to say and do comes in many forms:

- What should I ask?
- How do I know what to focus on?
- How active should I be?
- What techniques should I use?
- When do I speak and when do I keep quiet?
- When should I make an interpretation?
- What intervention should I use?

The specific answers to these questions depend on your theoretical orientation and your conceptualization of the client with whom you are working. In general, it will be your theoretical knowledge that will help you to know how to understand what you are experiencing, to develop hypotheses about diagnosis and treatment, and to generate ideas about what to do next.

Consider Greg, a young man who comes to you suffering

from moderate depression and social isolation. Depending on your theoretical orientation, this one symptom could activate many different ideas, strategies, and tactics. A psychodynamic therapist might first think of early shame experiences that led to a negative self-image and low self-esteem; a cognitive behavioral therapist would focus on negative self-statements that trigger and perpetuate Greg's depression; a family systems therapist may see the client's depression as an aspect of family homeostasis and scapegoating; an existential therapist might look to an absence of meaning in Greg's life. These very different theoretical starting points will lead to different understandings of mental illness, mental health, how to use the therapeutic relationship, and which strategies and interventions to employ.

Factors common to all forms of therapy that produce positive outcomes include:

- The therapist's care, compassion, or empathic attunement
- A balance of nurturance and challenge
- A balance of comfort and stress
- A balance of affect and cognition
- A goal of increased affect regulation
- The cocreation of new narratives or the development of a new story about the self

Keeping these concepts in mind while working with Greg, I would first strive to develop a connection that communicates my caring for him as a person and my emotional attunement to his sadness and isolation. I would then try to balance this support with challenges to his negative self-concept, encourage him to share difficult personal material, or structure anxiety-provoking situations to confront some of his social fears. In our discussions, I would alternate challenge and support, all the while encouraging both the experience and articulation of emotion to help him increase his ability to tolerate higher levels of stress (with less distress).

All forms of treatment recognize the need for stress, from the subtle disruption of defenses created by the compassion of Carl Rogers, to facing the existential reality of death, to the exposure to fear-provoking stimuli of cognitive behavioral therapy for phobias. Learning the right balance of nurturance and stress for each client is a key challenge for therapists across orientations. Within this balance, the evocation of emotion coupled with the client's ability to put feelings into words is most likely to result in emotional growth, insight, and symptom reduction. This is one of Freud's essential insights and remains at the heart of psychotherapy regardless of theoretical orientation.

In psychotherapy, *understanding is the booby prize*. It is a hollow victory to end up with a detailed psychological explanation for problems that remain unchanged. On the other hand, the expression of emotion without conscious thought does not result in positive change either. Regardless of orientation, therapists will encourage clients overwhelmed with their feelings to think their way to solutions and help clients who are emotionally cut off to experience and express their feelings.

During this process, Greg and I would be developing a shared language that could come to serve as a new way for him to think about himself and his world. This "co-constructed" narrative should serve as a blueprint for future experience and behavior. How all of this plays out and the type of narrative Greg takes away from therapy will be highly dependent on my theoretical orientation.

Besides your theoretical orientation, the three primary theoretical tools that will guide you through therapy are your (1) case conceptualization, (2) treatment plan, and (3) case notes. These will ground you in your understanding of the process of therapy, how your theory applies to your client, and what to focus on from session to session. Supervision should provide you with these skills. The specifics will differ depending on your setting and supervisor, so stay flexible about the form and specific language. What is most important is to learn and understand the general principles you can apply throughout your career in a variety of situations.

Case Conceptualizations

A case conceptualization is the application of your theoretical orientation to your client. It provides a way of understanding the causes and cures of psychological distress and a rationale for your treatment strategies. It places the causes, effects, and complications of your client's difficulties in a theoretical framework that creates a guidance mechanism for therapy.

A case conceptualization includes:

- A description of presenting problems, symptoms, and possible diagnoses
- A theory or theories accounting for how and why the problems have arisen and evolved over time
- A general description of how problems are addressed and cured

Psychological problems usually arise from interactions between biological and social variables. Suboptimal parenting, stress, trauma, and metabolic disorders can lead to mental distress. Psychodynamic, cognitive behavioral, and other perspectives offer hypothetical explanations of how problems arise, how they are maintained, and how they can be cured. Your case conceptualization is based on utilizing one or more of these perspectives to link your clients' difficulties to a treatment plan focused on particular goals.

Say you decide to treat Greg from a cognitive behavioral orientation. You might start by giving him the Beck Depression Inventory to measure the level of his depression. You would assess him for suicidality, do a brief genogram to see if depression runs in his family, and discuss the possibility of an evaluation for antidepressant medication. Next you would examine his thoughts about himself, the world, and his future, as well as make a detailed assessment of his daily activities. Strategies would include modifying his negative cognitions and encouraging him to engage in behaviors that would provide him with positive social experiences to work against the depressive effects of isolation and inactivity. Your interactions with him would be proactive and structured, you would give him homework assignments and measure his progress on objective scales and behavioral charts. The overall goals would be to reduce the levels of both his depression and social isolation.

Treating Greg from a psychodynamic perspective might look quite different. You would still assess him for suicidality and you might make a referral for a medication consultation. Beyond these basics, you would provide a less structured relationship and be less active in guiding therapy. You might assume that Greg's depression was a function of early developmental difficulties related to trauma or attachment difficulties, and you would encourage him to talk about his childhood, his relationships, and how he experiences being in therapy. You would ask Greg to discuss his feelings about you, to share his dreams, to make free associations, and discuss his fantasies. In assessing the success of therapy, you would be most interested in whether Greg feels as if he is developing in a positive way.

As you can see from these two approaches to the same case, your theoretical conceptualization can result in differences in how therapy is conducted, the content discussed, and the client's experience of the relationship. There are few generic answers to questions about what to do because the answers depend on your theoretical orientation. I encourage you to participate in training that includes conceptualizing your clients from multiple theoretical orientations. Always take a crack at formulating a case conceptualization and don't be discouraged if it is difficult or confusing at first—this takes time and practice. The case conceptualization is your road map; don't be one of those people who refuses to ask for directions.

Treatment Plans

Like the case conceptualization, your treatment plan will be grounded in your theoretical orientation. Working backward from the goals developed with your client, design your interventions to lead to your goals. Your treatment plan connects your interventions with your goals through gradually increasing levels of challenge that approach the goals of treatment. Therapeutic progress is measured by attaining the successive goals that guide treatment.

Part of Greg's treatment plan includes increased socialization. The goal may be to have him participate in social activities three times a week. As prerequisites to this goal, the treatment plan may include assertiveness training, a referral for group therapy, and teaching him relaxation techniques that he can use when socializing. It may also include him calling at least one friend each day to decrease his isolation and provide him with people with which to socialize when he is ready. The general measure of Greg's progress in the area of socializing might be the number of social contacts he engages in per week.

Because you want to minimize failure experiences for your client, you break down the steps to goals into manageable components. A failure to attain a step may be a failure on your part to recognize an intermediate step that first needed to be accomplished. Taking responsibility for such failures can also reassure the client. If Greg attains the goal of going to a social gathering but is so anxious that he spends most of the time frozen in fear, then it is clear that his anxiety needed to be addressed first. In this way, "failures" can be reframed as "experiments" that provide valuable information for future progress.

Case Notes

Case notes should be brief and to the point. Although they are usually confidential, there is always the possibility that a client might read them or they may be opened for legal reasons. I suggest that case notes remain brief and avoid unnecessary and potentially embarrassing personal details. Certainly all emergency issues related to threat and danger need to be included. Keep track of the general content discussed, sessions both kept and canceled, and lateness and payment, because all of these factors may have therapeutic significance. Beyond these basics, the content of your case notes will depend on your theoretical orientation and what you are tracking. Because different clinical settings have a variety of standards for case notes, make sure you learn and comply with these expectations.

Greg's case notes would include an outline of his treatment plan, the accomplished steps along the way, roadblocks to progress, and other relevant reactions. Use your notes to keep track of both the goals and the steps to these goals. A brief glance at your case notes before a session should ground you in the current aspects of a client's therapy. This is especially important when you get to the point where you see many clients each week.

Sometimes I write my notes in a way that allows me to share them with my client. This is especially important when working with clients who are distrustful or paranoid. When a client expresses concern about what I think of them or what is in my file, I simply hand him my notes. When he sees that they correspond completely with what I've discussed with him, he relaxes and seldom asks to see my notes a second time. This can be a good way to build trust.

Given that all of us can take our progress for granted, being reminded of where we have come from can be encouraging and inspiring. Notes can be organized in such a way as to chart clients' progress to provide them with a sense of accomplishment. You can also keep records *with* the client in the form of charts, graphs, and lists of statements that serve as a log of steps toward the goals of therapy. These sorts of case notes enhance the sense of collaboration with clients, and inviting them to keep records with you is an indication of your respect for their capabilities and potential.

The Catch-22

Beginning therapists struggle to link theory and practice. When we first begin to see clients, the theoretical and practical aspects of psychotherapy reside in two separate areas of the brain that have a hard time communicating with each other. Training programs offer some classes on theory and others on clinical practice and expect outside supervisors to connect them. The catch-22 is that many outside supervisors assume that the students have learned to integrate theory and practice in the classroom. Students, not knowing any better, assume that they were supposed to have learned what supervisors assume they should know. Many students come to feel that there is something wrong with them and keep their ignorance a secret. I kept faking it and changing the subject for quite a while until I finally gave up the charade.

Try to avoid this catch-22. Make a point of learning theory, practice, and the integration of the two. The combining of theory and practice is a separate skill set that requires lots of guidance and repetition. Encourage your supervisor to be specific about the application of their theoretical orientation to case conceptualization, treatment, and record keeping. If you find that this integration is not included in your classes and that your supervisors are too busy or unable to provide you with this training, seek it out from other faculty, readings, and workshops. It won't just be difficult to be a competent, successful therapist without these skills and abilities—it will be impossible.

CHAPTER FOUR

Survival Strategies

Stories have to be told or they die, and
when they die, we can't remember who
we are or why we're here.

—SUE MONK KIDD

A FEW YEARS AGO I was giving a presentation about mental illness to a group of schizophrenic clients and their families. My hour-long talk included a description of symptoms, medications, and various forms of available treatment. After I was done with my talk, I took some questions, the group had a brief discussion, and we ended for the evening. As I was putting away my notes, one client came up, vigorously shook my hand, and said, "Good job, Doc. You're just a suppository of information!" He then spun on his heels and left.

At first I thought this might be a loose association. Then I began to suspect that he was telling me where I could put my "expertise" concerning *his* illness. Regardless of his true intent, whenever I begin to take myself too seriously, remembering that I am a suppository of information helps me to put things into perspective.

We do serious work. At times it can overwhelm us. Too often we are left to discover the risks and pitfalls of the profession on our own. Therefore, it is helpful to begin training with some strategies to increase our chances of having long and enjoyable careers. Following are a few "survival strategies" that I have found to be particularly helpful.

Don't Panic in the Face of the Pathology

When I reflect on my past experiences, the clinical situations that have most challenged my ability to remain calm and centered have involved the following:

- Suicidal threats and behaviors
- Self-mutilation
- Child sexual or physical abuse
- The reporting of traumatic experiences
- Dealing with a client's sexual interests and/or advances
- Bizarre psychotic beliefs

If you are facing any of these you need to remember survival strategy Number One: Don't panic! A competent clinician remains competent in the face of these kinds of challenges. Anxiety is the enemy of rational problem solving, and panic leads even experienced clinicians to operate from survival reflexes instead of therapeutic knowledge.

Clients with painful experiences and frightening symptoms are accustomed to living in a world where others avoid and reject them. Our ability to remain empathically connected to them through the expression of their suffering sets the stage for therapy to be a qualitatively different relationship experience—one where they are accepted, pain and all. Whether they are telling stories of their traumas or acting out their struggles in the therapeutic relationship, remaining centered, attentive, and connected is the foundation of our ability to provide a healing relationship.

Another reason not to panic is more subtle and more profound. Victims of trauma and abuse often find that sharing their experiences is extremely upsetting to listeners, so much so that they end up having to take care of the very people who are supposed to be taking care of them. Many victims report that others can't tolerate knowing what they have been through and, sadly, this is often true. Victims learn to edit or silence themselves to avoid upsetting others, being rejected, and having to cope with the emotional reaction their victimization engenders. Not telling their story is the most untherapeutic outcome possible. By not panicking, you allow your clients to share their painful experiences, which frees them from slipping into the familiar but untherapeutic caretaker role.

One of my first clients was a young man named Shaun. He had a flair for the dramatic and would stride around the consulting room making grand gesticulations while wrapping his problems in eloquent words. On one occasion, he threw open the window and sat on the sill. He took the cord from the blinds, performed some clever knot making, and came up with a perfect hangman's noose. He dangled the noose from his hand, swinging it back and forth like an executioner. Every so often he would look over to check out my reaction to his nonverbal communication. Alternately, he would lean out the third-story window to the point where most of his torso hung outside.

This was my first clinical panic. I thought, "Oh, great, I'm going to be known as the intern with the client who jumped out the window during a session. There will probably be a famous lawsuit with my name on it. How will *that* look in my evaluations?!" Each time his head disappeared out the window, I turned around to look at the one-way mirror, behind which my supervisor and other students were observing the session. With the expressiveness of a tragic opera character, I mouthed the word "help!"

In his wisdom, my supervisor chose not to intervene, and Shaun, fortunately, never jumped out the window. I later came to realize that Shaun was testing my ability to cope with his behaviors; he knew he was a handful. He wanted to see if I had the courage and centeredness to remain calm and stick with him in ways that his family and friends could not.

Over the years, I have had to deal with clients showing up at my door with gashes in their wrists, fathers threatening violence because I reported them for abusing their children, and tales of the most depraved human behaviors (the latter while working with victims of political torture and sadistic child abuse). Clients have had seizures, gone into diabetic comas, and experienced long and painful flashbacks during sessions. Although I haven't always known the best thing to do, I always remember survival strategy Number One—don't panic. If I don't panic, I can think about what is happening and what I can do.

Experience counts. The more you deal with situations like this, the easier it is to stay calm. Part of this is developing a "memory for the future"—meaning that, over time, we become accustomed to facing frightening and dangerous situations, which are followed by conscious problem solving and good outcomes. Repetitive experiences like this form an emotional memory that we have access to in crisis situations and that reminds us that things will work out.

In addition to a growing sense of confidence, it also helps to have crisis-situation action plans prepared in advance. For example:

- Early in supervision, discuss with your supervisor, in detail, what you should do in case of various emergencies such as when a client is a danger to himself or others.
- Put emergency phone numbers, including your supervisor's, on speed dial.
- Schedule potentially problematic or dangerous clients for times when your supervisor or other backup professionals are present.
- Alert others around you when you are meeting with a client who makes you uneasy so that they are on alert and can serve as backup if needed.
- Pay attention to your subtle feelings and instincts about a client and discuss them in supervision.

Expect the Unexpected

Never underestimate the value of preparation in being able to successfully deal with crises and problem situations. This leads to survival strategy Number Two: Expect the unexpected. When extreme situations do arise, keep some of the following principles in mind:

- Don't catastrophize. A client's strong emotions such as angry outbursts and uncontrollable sobbing tend to shift in a matter of a minute or two.
- Maintain boundaries. If a client has a feeling, it does not mean you also have to have it.

- Stay centered. If you sit calmly, it will provide a sense of safety and calm to your client.
- Provide structure. When a client is emotionally out of control, it is often helpful to provide gentle but firm instructions, such as "I think it would be helpful if you would sit down and focus on your breathing—let's do it together."
- Provide hope. While understanding your client's feelings, also remind him or her that things will get better. Many clients find hope in the fact that you have helped others with problems similar to theirs. Tell them stories of clients similar to them who had positive outcomes.
- Discuss strengths and resources. It is easy to forget our strengths, resources, and accomplishment when in a crisis. Taking a couple of minutes to discuss these at the end of a difficult session not only provides hope but also yields clues for additional interventions, such as the reestablishment of relationships and activities that have been forgotten during difficult periods.

I received a call on a Sunday morning with a request that I meet a young girl for an emergency consultation that afternoon. When I arrived at my office, I found Sandy slumped down in a chair, looking half asleep and half in shock. She looked so emaciated, her color so bad, that I felt immediate concern for her physical health. Once in my office she told me in an emotionless tone that she thought that she had been raped the night before in a parking lot outside of a nightclub. She was home for a week from her East Coast prep school and had gone out dancing with some friends. As was her habit, she had drunk to the point of unconsciousness, so she couldn't recall whether the sex she had was consensual or not.

Sandy's words flowed like water from a cracking dam; she wanted and needed to tell me everything on her mind and in her heart. She described a long history of bulimia, cocaine use, binge drinking, a number of serious automobile accidents, failing grades at school, and her victimization at the hands of numerous boyfriends. Sandy also told me of her loveless childhood and her parents' sending her off to boarding schools from a very young age. She spoke for almost 90 minutes and I didn't interrupt because I sensed her need to finally share all of her pain with someone who might be able to help.

Sandy said that she had "half a dozen" problems, many diagnoses, needed to be in several support groups, and felt that there was no hope for her. What had happened to her the night before wasn't atypical for her; what *was* different was her feeling of hopelessness and thoughts of suicide. After this, she became silent, glanced over at me, sat back into the couch, and gave me a look that said, "Okay, your turn." I was so immersed in her story and so impressed with her emptiness and pain that it took me a while to turn my attention to what I would say.

Sandy's life clearly felt out of control. What I wanted to do was to take all that she had told me and to present it back to her in a way that demonstrated to her that I had heard what she said, understood the depth of her suffering, and could provide a perspective and plan that would give her hope of having a better life. I thought about all she had told me and came up with some ideas. This is what I told her: "Sandy, although it feels like you have many different problems, it seems to me that you have one core struggle—the need to feel loved and cared for." I thought that this might be correct because I could see Sandy's posture change as the first tears poured from her eyes. "My sense is that although your eating disorder, alcohol and drug use, and bad relationships all seem like different problems, they may all be attempts to cope with the loneliness and anxiety you feel every day. Even your car accidents, where you drive your new car into a tree, may be a way to tell your parents something is wrong. With each accident, instead of hearing your pain, they only have another car delivered to your school."

Having one central problem as opposed to "half a dozen" made Sandy feel a sense of hope. She took off time from school and I began to work with her and her family around issues of attachment, bonding, parenting, caring, and love. Sandy's family wasn't ideal for her but she needed to learn that many of her parents' emotional inadequacies were not because she was unlovable but because of their own limitations. They needed to learn that their daughter needed more than money from them and Sandy had to learn a healthier way of asking for what she needed.

Crisis as Communication

As with Sandy, crises are often forms of communication—ways of communicating when words can't be found or aren't heeded. Many clients struggle with suicide and there are few clinical situations more difficult to deal with. Suicidal acts, gestures, and ideation make us concerned for our clients and ourselves. We are all told that we have a duty to protect our clients, but what is the best way to do this and still preserve the therapeutic relationship and the client's confidentiality? These are difficult clinical situations that we learn to cope with but never get easy.

Roberta had been depressed for years. She told me that every few years she would try to kill herself in ways that were fairly lethal. Over the years, Roberta had come to understand that her suicidal actions were desperate attempts to gain the love and attention that she never felt she was given by her parents, siblings, or friends. Although it was clear to me that she wanted to live, I was concerned that she would someday miscalculate these calls for help and accidentally kill herself.

One afternoon, she came to my office with a clear plan to commit suicide later that evening. As she described her detailed plan of getting a gun, going down into her basement, and setting the stage for her death, I grew more and more frightened. Her description was so detailed, I could vividly picture every stage of the process. I raced through options in my mind: barring her from leaving my office, calling the police, taking her to a hospital, and so on. I tried not to panic, stay calm, and think through the logistics, complications, and risks of these options. All of the interventions that came to mind had been done by Roberta's previous therapists and had led to her ending each relationship. Was there something else I could do?

Still struggling to remain calm, I asked Roberta what she hoped to accomplish by attempting suicide. As she spoke, it became clear that she wanted her brother to know how alone and hurt she felt. She wanted him to feel guilty for not paying better attention to her. This soon flowed into a discussion of her wanting me to know these things about her inner experience and my empathic shortcomings. Roberta somehow felt that a suicide attempt was the only way she could make me understand the intensity of her pain.

By the end of the session, I had somehow assured her that

I understood the depth of her suffering and why she would commit suicide, but that a suicide attempt (as a form of communication) would be redundant to what I already knew. I also assured her that I wanted our relationship to continue and that her past hospitalizations always resulted in so much shame that she discontinued her work with her therapist. Roberta and I made a standard suicide contract and scheduled extra meetings to help her through this difficult time. For me, the most important aspect of this session was my ability to avoid panicking, remember my training, stay in the role of a therapist, and hang in there with Roberta's experience.

Don't Try to Reason with an Irrational Person

This is survival strategy Number Three. It will save you hours of wasted energy and keep you from missing the important emotional realities behind much irrational behavior. Although we can generally rely on reason to aid us in finding solutions to complex problems, it doesn't always work. Some people have such a firm image of what is true that they cannot be swayed by reason. The emotional circuits of the brain are easily capable of inhibiting or overriding rational thought; some clients only see things that fall in line with their prejudices and beliefs. Those fighting with God on their side seldom stop to think about the god leading their enemies into battle.

For a number of years I worked in a hospital ward with actively psychotic individuals. I saw clients in both individual and group therapy and participated in many ward activities. During a session with a woman named Wanda, I became aware that she believed she was a few months pregnant. In discussion with the nurses, I was assured that this could not possibly be the case and that Wanda was suffering from a delusional belief. It made no difference that the nurses had told this to Wanda; she remained steadfast in her belief that she would soon be a mother.

To complicate things even more, during one of our sessions, Wanda revealed to me that she was pregnant with a cat! I liked cats, but this one caught me by surprise—I still hadn't learned to expect the unexpected—and I decided that I definitely needed to do something. I suggested that she bring this belief up in group therapy later that day, assuming that when the other group members heard her story, they would help Wanda to realize the impossibility of her belief.

Based on my suggestion, she waited her turn in group and made her joyous announcement. Although there were some doubters at first, by the end of the hour Wanda had convinced the group that it *was* possible for a woman to become pregnant by a male cat if the conditions were right. Amazed and impressed by her skills of persuasion, I nevertheless refused to give up my reality campaign. After the group meeting, I asked the nurse to schedule a pregnancy exam so that Wanda could hear from a physician that she was not pregnant. That had to work!

The next week Wanda came back from her pregnancy test just beaming! She told everyone that she had been to the doctor and was happy to announce that her kitten was doing fine. In fact, she had even spotted a few whiskers during the pelvic exam. The group began planning a kitten shower and, under some pressure, I agreed to contribute a litter box. The nurses cried with laughter when I told them about the kitten shower my group was planning for Wanda. They had learned long ago not to argue with Wanda's delusional beliefs. Apparently, I was not the first intern who had tried to get her to engage in "reality testing." Wearing a sympathetic smile, one of the nurses suggested that I might have bumped up against the limits of psychotherapy.

We run into irrational beliefs all the time. The chronic alcoholic client will insist he can drink in moderation; the emaciated anorectic client will adamantly claim to be obese. Rather than feeling compelled to impose your reality, sit back and discover what the world looks like through their eyes. Be patient and understanding. As most people go through the process of therapy, they steadily reevaluate their beliefs with gentle, strategic, and well-timed doses of reality. As Wanda demonstrated, "in your face" reality testing doesn't always work. Even very delusional clients often realize that their reality differs from yours. Your empathic availability may do more to bring them to consensual reality than any rational argument, and it will protect you from feelings of frustration that may be counterproductive.

Instead of trying to impose my reality on Wanda, I needed to learn that, despite her mental illness, she desired to be loving and nurturant. Wanda was coping with other realities— separation from her family, getting older, and never having children of her own. Her needs to nurture and be fulfilled as a woman were the eventual foci of therapy, as they should have been from the beginning. She needed to take her medication on a regular basis so she could be home with her family, and her family needed to know how to care for her illness. Perhaps now I would have started therapy by going to the animal shelter and getting Wanda a kitten.

Don't Forget a Client's Strengths

After you've spent years in classes focusing on abnormal psychology, diagnosis, and treatment, it is easy to see pathology in every action and behavior. But, as Freud suggested, not every cigar is a phallic symbol. Because people are coming to therapy for their problems, it is easy for both client and therapist to get tunnel vision and forget to see the positive aspects of their lives. If your client has struggled with anxiety, depression, or trauma for a long period of time, he or she may have lost sight of the people, accomplishments, and good things in his or her life.

In your quest to diagnose and treat pathology, remember that every client possesses at least one strength. Whether that strength is a musical talent, the love of a pet, or a burning passion to ride motorcycles, it may boost self-esteem or motivate change. A desire to see lions in their natural habitat—or to show up a high school counselor who said they would never amount to anything—can be used as leverage to take on new challenges and inspire new behaviors.

Describing resources and strengths may help to put the problems you plan to focus on in perspective. Keep in mind, however, that this needs to be done with great care. You run the risk of having your client think that you are not taking their problems seriously and that you want to avoid their negative feelings. They may actually have a point if, based on your discomfort with their troubles, you try to steer the therapy in a way that communicates to them "just look at the bright side" or "keep a stiff upper lip." With this caution in mind, try to balance your attention to "problems" with attention to "strengths."

I have been pleasantly surprised on a number of occasions at the positive results I've gained from encouraging (and sometimes even harassing) clients into describing their strengths. I've found that encouraging clients to review their past accomplishments, positive relationships, interests, hobbies, and passions will actually lift their spirits. Having them reconnect with activities of interest as soon as possible in the process of therapy can also enhance their receptivity to what is focused on during sessions. When people feel sad and guilty, they often deprive themselves of positive experiences. If you prescribe these as part of the therapy, they may feel less guilty about doing them and rationalize their enjoyment as "doctor's orders."

CHAPTER FIVE

Beware of Assumptions

Two things are infinite, the universe and
human stupidity.
—ALBERT EINSTEIN

EVERY THERAPY SESSION provides countless
opportunities for us to be ignorant and to practice not knowing. Each client has a life history, a set of experiences, and a
way of using language that we come to know gradually as our
relationship deepens and grows. Beginning therapists,
unnerved by their lack of experience, often try to cover up
their ignorance and don't ask vital questions for fear of sound-
ing stupid. It may help to realize that your admission of ignorance, genuine questions, and desire to learn about your
client is most often experienced as interest and caring, not
incompetence. Whether it is done as an unconscious reflex or
an attempt to be cool, making assumptions about our clients
can lead us down some unproductive and dangerous paths.

One of my professors spelled the word *assume* as "ASSume"
to remind us of the perils of making assumptions. Doing so
has certainly made an ass of me. One example that comes to

mind is when I assume that my clients and I have the same definition for a word. When a client tells me he has had "a drink," the image that comes to my mind is a can of beer, a glass of wine, or a mixed drink, about the size that would be served at a bar. I have found that for one client, a drink meant two bottles of wine; for another, it was a quart of vodka. I've learned to ask very specific questions when it comes to alcohol consumption.

One of my first clients was a young college student. His mother referred him to therapy because she felt his drinking was getting out of control. Joe was drinking about 12 cans of beer a day: a few for lunch and the rest in the evening. He was listless and unmotivated, his grades were poor, and he missed classes due to hangovers and apathy. He had become indifferent to his friends and rarely attended family events, choosing to stay alone in his apartment. Joe's case was complicated by his problematic relationship with his father and other negative family dynamics. After about a year of therapy, he had successfully stopped drinking and we were able to work through some of the issues in his family. Despite this, he still seemed listless and unmotivated.

Near the end of one memorable session, Joe was feeling better and reflecting on his progress. I will never forget him sitting back on the couch and proudly saying, "Yep, Doc, it sure is great to not be drinking anymore. I couldn't have done it without you and the marijuana." My eyes widened. "The marijuana?" I asked. Apparently he had compensated for his decreased drinking by increasing his daily use of marijuana. I was stunned. I had never asked about marijuana! His mother said he had a drinking problem and that was what I had focused on. You can imagine how I felt for having made that

ASSumption. Apparently, I'm not alone in this mistake. A colleague told me that one of her clients was in psychoanalysis for 15 years and never told her analyst she was an alcoholic. Why? Because she never asked.

Remember that asking a simple question is often not enough and what you are told isn't always true. People tend to forget or underestimate the things they are ashamed of and overestimate and inflate those things that make them feel better. Men tend to overestimate the number of sexual partners they have had whereas women do the opposite. Sometimes clients simply lie, confabulate, or fail to mention vital information. In our effort to be supportive, we tend to accept what they say. Although our intentions may be good, the consequences can be disastrous.

Child discipline is another area where asking specific questions is vital. Slapping, spanking, scolding, and time-outs have been used as euphemisms for punching, burning, kicking, and locking children in closets. Not only is there a problem of what the words mean, there is our resistance to hearing about adults treating children in such horrible ways. I force myself to ask about these details over the voices in my head saying, "Don't ask and they won't tell."

One of my clients, a man, described disciplining his children as "resetting their clocks." My assumption was that discussions with his children resulted in changes in their attitudes and behaviors. After he used the term a few times, I innocently asked what it meant. I discovered that resetting a child's clock consisted of sneaking up on them and hitting them on the side of the head with a piece of wood hard enough for them to lose (or nearly lose) consciousness. According to my client, this "reprogrammed" their thinking and behavior in a more positive direction. He was surprised by my surprise; after all, this was how his father raised him and, as he later stated, "look how good I turned out." He was even more surprised when I told him I had to file a child abuse report.

Areas where assumptions should always be questioned and explored in detail include:

• Alcohol and drug use
• Sexual behavior, especially in children and adolescents
• Disciplinary practices
• Past diagnoses from charts and medical records
• Cultural and religious values and beliefs

Assumptions are often based in countertransference. We may prefer not to know the truth or we may be too afraid to anger our clients by asking for clarification of potentially uncomfortable issues. Asking these questions requires the courage to experience the negative feelings in us and to tolerate the possible negative reaction of our clients.

Cultural and Religious Assumptions

An especially dangerous situation for making assumptions arises in work with people from other cultures. Feelings, behaviors, beliefs, the meaning of individuality, and the significance of disclosing personal information vary from culture to culture. Consider these questions that may arise in therapy:

• Does a daughter move away from her family before she is married?

- How much abuse does a wife tolerate from her mother-in-law?
- Does the son of migrant workers accept a scholarship to college?
- How close a relationship between a mother and son is healthy?
- How do we discuss sexual behaviors with adolescents from families with conservative religious beliefs?
- Should a client get an abortion or keep her baby?

These are all tricky situations for a therapist, requiring a great deal of information gathering, sensitivity, and care. It is all too easy to forget a "client-centered" approach and become an unconscious advocate for your own values and beliefs. It may be obvious to you that a young man should go to college, that no person should tolerate abuse from anyone, and that adolescents should be free to explore their sexuality, but your clients and their families may have very different beliefs.

Early in my training, Kim, a Korean woman in her early twenties, came to therapy suffering from symptoms of depression, anxiety, and exhaustion. She complained of getting low grades in school, feeling like a failure compared to her "brilliant" brothers, and being unattractive to men. Kim was the youngest of six children and the only girl in an extended family that included her mother and father, five brothers, maternal grandparents, and an aunt and uncle. Her mother and father worked long hours in the family store and all her brothers were in college.

As I came to learn about her day-to-day life, I was amazed to find that she was expected to do most of the housework and cooking while simultaneously attending college full-time. Because of her age and gender, she was at the disposal of everyone in her family. Despite all she did, she was criticized for her less-than-perfect grades and the fact that she was still single. Simultaneously, the family appeared to sabotage her attempts at socializing by coming up with new responsibilities for her when she was invited to social events or asked out on a date.

The more I learned, the more upset I became. Her acceptance of this kind of treatment made me impatient and angry. The stronger my feelings became, the less I discussed the case with my supervisor. I felt confident that I knew what I was doing precisely because I had such strong feelings about it. I fantasized about going to her home and yelling at everyone in the family to treat Kim with more care and respect. It was like having Cinderella as a client, but instead of two evil stepsisters, she had eleven people she was expected to wait on hand and foot. I wanted to help Kim escape her prison and have an independent life where she could nurture herself.

Over the 2 months that Kim came to therapy, I did everything wrong. I encouraged her to stand up to her family, decline many of the responsibilities placed on her, and look for her own apartment. When I grilled her on what she was doing to become more independent, she would describe some tentative, hesitant attempts at speaking up to her family that only resulted in their becoming angry and giving her more to do. Disregarding this, I would then encourage her to go back and try again. Of course she terminated therapy.

Instead of giving her the understanding and comfort she needed, I had become yet another authority figure demanding the impossible. Even worse, I was making suggestions that were completely inappropriate given her family and culture. She was too respectful to tell me that I didn't know how to help her. Instead, she dropped out of therapy and most likely came to the conclusion that there was no help for her.

What should I have done? There were many ways to reach a better outcome in this situation. The first would have been to take my strong feelings as an indication that I was having a countertransference reaction. Instead of talking less about this client in supervision, I should have discussed her more. Second, I should have spent time having Kim educate me about her family and cultural beliefs and sought consultation with therapists of Kim's background to help me learn what interventions would be culturally appropriate. And third, I should have understood not just how hard it must have been for her to come to therapy, but how she needed to please me as an authority figure. By foisting my countertransference onto Kim, I not only missed the opportunity to help her, but also made her feel more alone and helpless than before she came to therapy. Twenty years later, I still think of her and wish I had done a better job.

Some of the points I learned from working with Kim included:

- Strong feelings can indicate countertransference.
- Discuss feelings about a client in your supervision (and therapy).
- Think about how your client's problems and conflicts may relate to your own.
- Examine your assumptions and prejudices about your client's culture.

No One Is an Expert on Culture

No one person is an expert on culture. Cultures vary greatly, as do subgroups within cultures, based on economic status, education, and degree of acculturation. Furthermore, each family embodies the broader culture in a unique way and transmits it differently to its children. No matter how much you know about a particular culture, each individual's embodiment of his or her culture needs to be discovered in the therapy.

The good news is that we are off the hook; there is just too much knowledge to master. Our responsibility is to gain cultural sensitivity and stay aware of the potential importance of culture in the process of case management, diagnosis, and treatment. Cultural differences cannot be reduced to a set of clichés learned in a weekend seminar. Interacting with people from other cultures is an excellent opportunity to embrace your ignorance and practice a stance of not knowing. While practicing not knowing, keep these points in mind:

- Make your assumptions and prejudices conscious.
- List them and discuss them with colleagues.
- Make the decision that you are ignorant and need to learn about the culture.
- Ask the client to educate you about their culture.
- Consult with therapists and others from the culture to put your client's thoughts in perspective.
- Evaluate your diagnosis, case management, and treatment plan for appropriate cultural fit.
- Continue to stay open to adjusting your work as you expand your knowledge.

Anxiety about being "politically correct" leads us to hesitate to discuss sensitive cultural issues because we are afraid of saying something wrong or being offensive. This is the worst possible way to deal with unconscious assumptions. Without words and discussion, thoughts and feelings remain embedded in our unconscious. If we remain silent, we run the risk of carrying the cultural barriers of everyday life into the therapeutic relationship. Err on the side of openness in the areas of cultural differences and be ready to apologize if your ignorance does upset your client.

Not everything can be reduced to cultural differences. Psychological struggles and mental illness know no cultural boundaries. People can be emotionally disturbed no matter what their cultural, ethnic, or religious background. Their disturbances may merely look or sound different than we are accustom to. On the other hand, it is important not to mistake cultural differences for mental illness. People with different religious beliefs may sound psychotic based on their beliefs in the supernatural, how they think about God, or their relationships with deceased relatives. What looks like resistance may be suspiciousness based on centuries of prejudice and oppression. Those with "unusual" moral and ethical standards may seem mentally unbalanced until we look more closely at their unique life experiences.

Prejudice Is Everywhere

Prejudice is everywhere, some obvious and some very subtle, occurring not just among groups of people but within groups as well. I have worked with therapists who are much more vulnerable to distortions and countertransference issues with clients from their own religious or racial group. The therapist's personal experiences with these issues can exert a positive and negative influence on the therapeutic relationship. Never assume prejudice does not exist between a client and therapist of the same group. Intra-group countertransference often goes emotionally deeper than inter-group prejudice.

For all of these reasons, allow clients who are culturally different from you to teach you about their culture before you draw any conclusions about their problems or psychological conditions. When discussing their lives, ask them to describe how some of their behaviors or symptoms are seen and understood by their family and understood within their culture. People from minority cultures are often so accustomed to being misunderstood that they don't even bother to mention how you are misattuned to their thoughts and feelings.

Try asking your clients some of the following questions to explore these areas:

- In what ways is it hard for you to make people of my culture understand you?
- Do you try to correct my mistakes about your culture or do you let them go?
- What do I understand about your culture and what do I seem to miss?
- Do our differences make it hard for you to correct my mistakes?
- Do I take culture into account enough in trying to understand you?
- Do I overemphasize your culture in our discussions or in my understanding of you?

Prejudices shared by a professional community can sometimes masquerade as science. In the 19th century, a Southern physician created two categories of mental illnesses that occurred only in slaves. Drapetomania caused slaves to run away and dysaethesia aethiopica resulted in slaves' wasting and destroying everything they handled. Well into the 20th century, hysteria was thought to be a problem particular to overly emotional women and caused by their uterus wandering through their bodies. Until recently, homosexuality was considered a psychiatric illness. Diagnosis as prejudice has a long and well-documented history; we need to be attentive to how our own biases may shape professional doctrine and our professional opinion.

The Shame of the Accused

I once worked with a man named Amfo, who was from a country in northwest Africa and who had been mistakenly arrested for robbing a bank. He was at the wrong place at the wrong time, arrested, brought in for questioning, and then set free with an apology. A short time after this experience, he experienced extreme shame, guilt, and even considered suicide. At first glance, it appeared that the stress of his encounter with the law may have triggered a severe depressive or psychotic reaction. From my own background and perspective, I would not have imagined that being wrongly accused and falsely imprisoned could result in such a severe psychological reaction. My first impulse would be to hire an aggressive attorney and retire on the financial settlement. I had to hold myself back from becoming Amfo's agent in a civil suit.

While getting to know Amfo, I asked him to educate me about his homeland. He was very pleased that I was interested. Talking about his home, family, and traditions seemed to lighten his mood and be therapeutic by itself. As part of my education, Amfo told me a story of a man from his country who had committed suicide because he had been wrongly accused of stealing an egg from a street market. I came to learn that in his culture, a sense of self and one's reputation were inseparable. Once your reputation had been tainted, rightly or wrongly, you became a "shadow man" or a type of ghost bringing shame on your family, your village, and your ancestors. It took me quite a while to fully grasp why Amfo felt so devastated. For Amfo, to be accused was a trauma that threatened his personal and social survival.

Amfo had never developed the thick skin needed to cope with being black in a white society. He experienced his treatment at the hands of the police as if he had been accused by the people of his village. In our work together, he learned to separate the accusations from his personal identity. Part of his treatment was learning more about the history of race relations in the United States and talking to African Americans about their experiences. This was a task we took on together.

To my mind, being culturally sensitive means that you accept your ignorance, find the information you need to do a good job, and continue to test what you have learned. When your client is from a culture other than yours, try not to worry about appearing stupid because you are asking to be educated. Most members of minority groups are accustomed to dealing with misunderstanding and prejudice. Your interest and admission of ignorance will almost always be experienced as a breath of fresh air. It will demonstrate both your desire to get to know your clients and your confidence in yourself.

PART TWO

Getting to Know Your Clients

CHAPTER SIX

Challenges and Strategies

> He maintained concentration, mindful-
> ness, and meditation in order to sustain
> the mentally troubled.
>
> —VIMALAKIRTI

CONGRATULATIONS! You've made it through your first sessions. I remember how much courage that takes, so give yourself plenty of credit. The scariest part is over! Now let's get down to work. Important learning occurs in the hours and days right after your first sessions, while the experiences are still fresh in your mind and body. The stress of these early sessions can actually prime your brain to grow in an acceler-ated fashion. This is why we should spend as much time as possible listening to taped sessions and seeking consultation in the early months of training. This is also why our first supervisors are so important.

In reviewing our sessions we can always find ways we could have done something better, see things we missed, and rec-ognize how we walked right into difficulties. Doubting our judgment and second-guessing our decisions comes with all complex endeavors. Doubt, if not taken to a paralyzing extreme, is a sign of an active mind and can keep us experimenting with new approaches. A therapist who is absolutely certain he or she is doing the right thing is a dangerous therapist. Psychotherapists don't deal in certainties but in educated guesses, intuition, and gut feelings. Embrace your uncertainty and keep in mind that psychotherapy is an art informed in equal measures by thought and emotion.

When you are reviewing a therapy session, begin by thinking about the things you did right. Don't be egotistical about it; just take a minute to list what you were able to accomplish. A good way to begin might be to answer the "Did I's?"

Did I:

- Show up on time, rested, centered, and prepared for the session?
- Review the relevant case notes before the session?
- Communicate a sense of caring and concern for my client?
- Listen actively?
- Allow my client to express him-or herself without interrupting?
- Deal with any emergency concerns appropriately?
- Establish an emotional connection?

These basic elements are the heart and soul of the therapeutic relationship and, according to clients, account for the most of the positive results they experience. I suggest that both you and your supervisor take a moment to give you credit for these and other basics you were able to accomplish. Check that you have covered these basics before focusing on what was discussed, the techniques you employed, or the deeper emotional subtext of the session.

While checking the basics, beware of the "Why Didn't I's?" Why Didn't I:

- Say more?
- Say less?
- Ask certain questions?
- Say certain things?
- Keep quiet?
- Not interrupt?

It is always easy to find mistakes when listening to taped sessions. It is much harder to spot them when you are caught up in the complex emotions during a session. Even the most experienced therapists second-guess themselves. Don't use second guesses to beat yourself up, rather, use them to think of new ways of being with clients in the future. If you knew everything, you would have no need to go to school!

The Value of Confusion

It is okay to be confused! Being confused with your client and collaborating in discovering answers can be an excellent approach to therapy. Genuine collaboration requires that you relinquish some control; this may be extremely difficult if you feel you need to be the one with all the answers. How you have responded to others in your personal relationships may yield important clues about your need for control, how you tend to maintain control, and your level of comfort with ambiguity and confusion. Ask friends and loved ones for feedback in these areas and listen carefully to what they tell you about yourself. Remember: Control is the enemy of exploration.

Confusion can also be useful as a conscious strategy. The role of a confused and befuddled detective can be far more effective than that of a brilliant spy (think Columbo rather than 007). Telling someone she's not making sense is far less helpful than telling her you don't understand. It is also easy to repeat back what she said as a question by raising your voice at the end of the sentence. Try some of these statements with your clients:

- I'm confused.
- Help me to understand what you mean.
- What do you mean when you say that?
- Could you say that again? I didn't quite follow.

Don't be afraid to tilt your head, wrinkle your brow, or look confused. It is far better to gently guide a client to self-insight than it is to tell him what he should be thinking. All we need to do in some cases is to listen and be willing to share our confusion. If your clients say things that are illogical or contradictory, asking them to explain these to you until they make sense is often much better than leaping to interpretations. The illogic may reveal itself and clients will make statements like, "Hearing myself saying this out loud makes me realize it doesn't make sense."

Beginning therapists tell me that they jump in with an interpretation because they are concerned about missing the opportunity to point out something to a client. I've found that the process of therapy (like the unconscious) is more circular than linear. You don't have to worry about missing an opportunity to deal with a particular perception or feeling; core aspects of a client's inner world permeate so many facets of his or her life that they are revealed in a multitude of situations. If an issue is important, it is bound to return. Seeing an issue repeatedly emerge will provide you with more confidence for a future interpretation. I will further discuss the basic elements of making interpretations later.

The Good-Enough Therapist

The pediatrician Donald Winnicott described the "good-enough mother" as one who is available, empathically attuned, and caring enough to help a child grow and thrive. He used "good-enough" to acknowledge that a mother need not be perfect to be a good mother. I suspect that he emphasized this concept to work against the guilt parents often feel about their failures and imperfections. Therapists share this failed struggle for perfection with parents. The fact that you will make many mistakes as a therapist is inevitable, so surrender to your imperfection. What you *do* have control over is how you deal with your mistakes and whether you are able to turn them to your client's advantage. Most mistakes don't end a therapeutic relationship; they become a part of its process and development.

As a boy, I was an avid chess player and loved to hear the professionals describe their strategies. When asked about the secret of his success, one chess master replied, "My strategy is to stay flexible and not become too attached to any particular game plan. Most importantly, when I have to retreat, I retreat to a better position." I was stunned by the beauty and profundity of this simple statement. I have applied this rule to many areas of my life, but it is especially relevant in therapy.

When I make a mistake or a client confronts me about something I've done wrong, my reflex is to become defensive, confused, or try to figure out how *they* must be wrong. I want to dive in immediately and attack the problem. This all-too-human reaction is hard to avoid. When these feelings occur, I have learned to stop, breathe, and keep quiet for a few moments. The challenge is to retreat, step back from this defensiveness, and try to understand what is happening in the therapeutic process. At the same time, I want to remain emotionally connected with the client. I have to remember not to let my emotions take control but to keep listening, remain flexible, and retreat to a better position.

I recently worked with a family attempting to organize their estate. The focus of attention was the dividing up of tens of millions of dollars to be passed from parents to children. The parents, their three adult children, and their spouses all had differing beliefs about how this should happen. Sorting out the family dynamics and economic realities was an intellectual challenge and, at times, I felt as if I were in the middle of a three-ring circus. As time went on, I grew increasingly impatient with their petty disagreements and became more authoritarian in my approach. I could see that this wasn't working, but, for some reason, I kept intervening in unhelpful ways.

Between sessions, one of the sons called me to say that he was unhappy with how I was working with the family. He said I seemed angry with all of them and I should think about what I was doing. I told him that I would give it some thought and quickly got off the phone. I was angry that he called and realized I was angry at the entire family. As I sat with these feelings, I recalled a similar feeling of how left out I felt when

I was a boy and my father remarried and started another family. Being with *this* family, yet not being included in a share of its resources, stimulated old feelings in me connected to being on my own, financially insecure, and on the outside looking in.

I shook my head as I found, once again, my unconscious affecting my work. I called the client back, apologized for being so abrupt when he called, and asked him to help me see my behavior from his perspective. In the days before our next meeting, I spent a great deal of time thinking about how to move from the role of abandoned child back into the role of therapist. I began to see how, in this family, money had always been substituted for love and that this was the real issue between husband and wife, parents and children. I suggested we put the discussion of the estate on hold and work on the emotional issues just below the surface. I felt like a therapist again.

Following are some things I try to keep in mind when I am confronted about making a mistake and have confused and defensive feelings:

- First, remember that to err is human.
- Try to listen in as nondefensive a manner as possible.
- Try to learn from your clients' experiences of your mistakes.
- Place a client's experience of you in the context of his or her history.
- Examine relevant countertransference issues in yourself.
- Ask yourself, "In what ways is my client correct?"
- Offer a genuine apology for the negative impact your behavior has had on your client.

Whether it is chess or therapy, suppose a situation has arisen that you failed to anticipate. If you focus on the mistake, become anxious and knocked off center, you will react out of anxiety or anger instead of from a place of compassion and good clinical judgment. In chess, this means compounding your initial error by putting additional pieces in jeopardy. In psychotherapy, it means taking the interpersonal distance created by your mistake and multiplying it by a dismissing or combative reaction. Your defensiveness will, in turn, only increase your client's defensiveness, resulting in a spiral of separation that will undermine the relationship and thwart progress.

Your goal is not to be right; it is to help your client move in the direction of psychological health. Being right is far less important than being caring, empathic, and available. Each client's defenses need to be understood and appreciated because they have helped him or her to survive. Clients need to be respected for their strength and courage in the face of what they have made it through. If your client feels that you appreciate the reason for his defenses, he will be more willing to explore alternative ways of being. Take care not to become attached to having the client buy into your agenda or see things from your point of view. The client is more important than *your* agenda. Be willing to let go of your opinions, interpretations, and suggestions and attend to where the client needs to take you. The more you push your agenda, the more the client will resist.

From time to time I'm caught by surprise by a client's strong emotional reaction to something I've said or done. Usually, I have an immediate defensive reaction that I need to check. My next step is to find out as much as I possibly can about what was experienced and understood by my client. If I fail to adequately manage my defensiveness, I run the risk of arguing, debating, and becoming attached to my position. Choosing your client's needs over your own emotions is an important moment in the therapeutic relationship. It presents the opportunity to demonstrate your skill, wisdom, and compassion.

If you find yourself arguing with your client, you have already lost. Remember, psychological defenses get stronger when under attack. Stop and rethink your strategy. You should quickly shift perspective to your client's point of view and try to understand, as quickly as possible, how he or she is right.

I almost never tell a client things like:

- I think you're resisting.
- You're kidding yourself.
- You can't handle the truth!

Instead, I say things like:

- I'm sorry I misunderstood.
- Tell me how you understand it.
- What have you found helpful in the past?

Join clients in their perspective, apologize for missing where they were coming from, and reconsider your assessment of the situation. See what they have to teach you about how they need to work. Here is a tricky part: A client can resist both by rebelling and by conforming, so beware of compliant clients. It is often more difficult to see resistance when someone seems to be agreeing with you and telling you how smart you are than when he or she is openly disagreeing.

Sometimes a difference in the definition of a word, a misunderstanding, or some other minor communication glitch is easily clarified. Sharon, a novelist in her forties, was describing her mixed feelings of respect and jealousy toward her friend Joyce. I responded by mirroring back what I thought she was telling me, so I could be sure I understood. Sharon's relaxed expression dramatically shifted to anger and then rage. "How dare you accuse me of envy!" she shouted. Crossing her arms in front of her, she sat in silence and stared at the floor. Sitting across from her, I found myself getting angry at her for being angry at me. We sat in silence until the time was up. She rose and left the room without a word.

She came for the next appointment in the same emotional state. After a few minutes, she looked up at me and asked, "How could you?" The only clue I had to go on was that she felt I had accused her of envy. "I can see you are very upset with me," I said, "and the only clue I have is that it has something to do with envy. Can you help me understand what you are feeling?" It turns out that I substituted the word envy for jealousy. For me, the meanings of these words are somewhat interchangeable, yet for Sharon, there was a world of difference. She understood jealousy as a relatively benign and childish emotion, whereas envy was a sin against God.

My use of the word envy had triggered memories of her years in a cultlike religious organization and her struggle to see herself as a worthy person. Fortunately, a clarification of how we both understood and used these words led us to a resolution of our conflict. I was certainly appreciative of the fact that I didn't react emotionally to Sharon's initial behavior and attempt to explain myself or pull out a dictionary to explain the meaning of both terms.

Making Good Mistakes

Each mistake is an opportunity to make a good mistake. It all depends on how you handle it. A good mistake provides a number of valuable opportunities:

- To increase your understanding by knowing how a client reacts to something you have said or done that has offended or hurt him or her.
- To deepen your connection with the client via your acceptance of their perceptions, feelings, and your ability to accept responsibility for what you have done.
- To allow them to experience a person of authority who does not have to always be right at their expense.
- To create an interpersonal context for your client to experience the cycle of rupture and repair within a sustained relationship.

The last point is especially important. Most clients have experienced a series of ruptured and unrepaired relationships. Many grow up with parents who are unable to admit their mistakes or shortcomings and have to find some way to blame everything on someone else. This communicates to a child that everything that goes wrong is a result of their imperfections. Shame, isolation, and anger are common reactions to these situations; you can provide an avenue of healing by being willing to take responsibility for problems in the therapeutic relationship. You can offer a willingness to ride out problems, continue to be concerned for them, and work diligently to repair breaks in your relationship. This takes patience, skill, and ongoing emotional availability. I try to remind myself that turning a mistake into a good mistake is a test of my maturity and an opportunity to enhance therapy.

I made a memorable mistake years ago that taught me the vital importance of paying close and consistent attention to my own emotional state. I was driving to the office one day and was stopped at a light behind a car filled with four elderly women. They were engaged in animated conversation, and I remember smiling at the fun they seemed to be having. After the light changed, they proceeded into the intersection and were broadsided by a speeding car. I discovered later that there had been a bank robbery and this was the getaway vehicle. The women in front of me were hit at such a high speed that the small car was literally cut in half. I watched in stunned horror as two of the women were hurled onto the pavement.

While most everyone's attention was on the two thieves, my eyes were fixed on one of the women lying face down on the street. I watched her lie still, move for a moment, and then become still again. After a while, someone went over to her and laid a blanket over her. I sat in my car staring at the body, flooded by images of the women talking moments before their death. I also realized that I could have just as easily been in her place had the robbers come through the intersection just a few seconds later.

When we were finally allowed to move from the scene, I went about my day, going to the office, doing paperwork, and seeing clients. Having no opportunity to talk to anyone about my experience, I coped with my upset and horror by staying busy. My last session of the day was with a very difficult client, a sensitive and hostile man who needed to be treated with a blend of careful compassion and patience that I was incapable of giving that evening.

I suspected that his narcissistic symptoms were a result of early childhood abandonment and empathic failures. My usual approach was to remain connected and supportive through these negative emotions in order to build a curative alliance and help him work through his early loss. His explosive emotions often got in the way of his relationships with others and he was desperate to learn how to create and sustain positive connections. During this particular session, I was not guided by my conceptualization or treatment plan. I experienced his entitlement and hostility as petty and self-centered. My mind kept going back to the accident while he complained about the small disappointments of an overprivileged life. My usual therapeutic stance toward him was replaced by hostility and insensitivity.

As the session progressed, he bristled at my impatience and lack of understanding, things he experienced from nearly everyone else in his life. By the end of the session, he was very angry and told me that he was not sure he would be returning next week. As he was leaving the office, I suggested that we talk about it during our next session while silently hoping he would never return. I stood in my office muttering under my breath as I watched him walk down the hall.

Later that evening, a friend asked me about my day. I began with various details before remembering the accident. As I described it to her, I was overwhelmed by the horrible images that came flooding into my mind and began to cry. I told her how horribly I felt for the women and how close I had come to dying. As I put these feelings into words, I realized how rigidly I was holding my body and how traumatized I felt. Only then was I able to think about my last session in light of my agitated, dissociated emotional state. I had obviously made a mistake by seeing him in this state of mind. The question now became, would I, could I, turn this into a good mistake?

The next day, I debated over whether or not to call him and discuss the session. I weighed the relative value of calling right away versus waiting until next week's session. The more uncomfortable I grew with the thought of us both sitting with these negative feelings for an entire week, the more I decided it would be best to call. I reached him that afternoon and told him a bit about my experience before our session of the previous day. I told him that I wished now that I had canceled our session, but had not realized at the time how upset the accident had left me. His response was quite hostile. Why hadn't I been aware of my feelings enough to know better than to have taken my problems out on him? He was 100% correct and I told him so. He agreed to discuss this further in our regular appointment.

Eventually, I was able to tie my bad behavior that day to mistakes my client had made in his relationships with family and friends. My irritability, his hurt feelings, and my apology eventually became a model for monitoring his own emotional state, its impact on others, and his ability to apologize for hurting other peoples' feelings. He came to see that there needs to be room in relationships to make mistakes, offer apologies, and allow for healing. We had held onto each other through a cycle of rupture and repair and I was able to use a good mistake for its therapeutic value.

Because of our fragile egos and our need to avoid feelings of shame, we all differ in our ability to admit when we are wrong. Receiving an honest and heartfelt apology is an all-too-rare experience. When it does happen, it can decrease our defensiveness and make us feel closer and more trusting of one another. Apologies can be therapeutic.

The Projective Hypothesis

Black holes are collapsed stars of incredible density and gravitational strength. In fact, their gravity is so strong that not even light escapes them. Although no one has ever seen a black hole, we know of their existence by the influence they exert on the stars, planets, and even the space around them. The unconscious is a lot like a black hole invisibly influencing our words, thoughts, and deeds.

Astronomers gaze at stars, planets, and comets; therapists explore behaviors, emotions, and thoughts, listening carefully to what is said and unsaid. Therapists study an individual's unconscious by examining such things as distortions of reality, incongruities between words and actions, and the origins and effects of psychological symptoms. Freud's projective hypothesis describes the process by which our brains unconsciously organize our experience of the world. The way we perceive and understand ambiguous stimuli (such as an ink blot or a new acquaintance) provides clues about our unconscious processes.

The therapist employs the projective hypothesis in a number of ways. By not giving the client much personal information, you yourself become a kind of ink blot. We try, as much as possible, to maintain this "neutral stance" in order to allow clients to project feelings and thoughts onto us. This form of projection, referred to as *transference,* results in the experiencing of emotions and expectations from earlier relationships within the therapeutic relationship. Because learning from early relationships is usually established before conscious memory is formed, transference allows access to otherwise hidden and unconscious learning. Through transference, the conflicts of early relationships are brought into therapy and can be worked on firsthand. The evocation and exploration of the transference can be a key component of successful psychotherapy.

As therapists, we are often less interested in answering clients' questions than we are in discovering the motivation for the question or what the imagined answers might be. Questions such as "Are you bored with listening to my problems?" or "I think you want to fire me from your practice" may contain a wealth of information about our client's unconscious. Although assuring a client that you don't have these feelings is important, you will first want to also explore these thoughts and feelings. If you are yawning or distracted, you may well look very bored. But more often, these statements reflect the client's past experiences and self-image, both of which are fertile grounds for exploration.

Transference is a form of projection where feelings from a previous significant relationship influence the client's perception of the therapist. Transference manifests in many forms. Following are some examples:

• A client who was dominated by his father may look to you for specific advice about what job to take, what car to buy, or how to dress.

- A woman who was abused as a child may be timid and frightened, avoid your gaze, and appear anxious for the session to end.
- A man who grew up having to take care of everyone around him in order to be accepted may bring you gifts, ask you about your health, and assure you that if you need to miss a session, he completely understands.

Projective tests are another tool at our disposal to circumvent client defenses that are working to keep unconscious material out of awareness. Tests like the Rorschach, the Thematic Apperception Test (TAT), or sentence-completion tasks present an ambiguous or incomplete stimulus to the client in order to reveal how he or she will organize the material.

I did psychological testing with a boy named Matthew. He had done fine in school until the beginning of the third grade, when his attention, concentration, and grades plummeted. Matthew had stopped participating in sports, withdrew from his friends, and gained enough weight to be considered obese. Extensive evaluations had revealed no underlying medical illness, and everyone was puzzled by what looked like a severe depression with no precipitant or family history of affective disorders. The only change in his life situation was that over the summer, his mother's boyfriend had moved in with Matthew and his mother.

His teacher had noticed bruises on Matthew's face and neck but assumed it had happened during rough-and-tumble play. As his teacher and mother began to compare notes, the question of abuse was raised. Despite the mother's denial, he was referred for testing to find out more about his depression and the possibility of abuse. During my interview with him,

Matthew was withdrawn and distracted. When I asked him late in the interview if he had ever been hit or hurt, he said "no" and quickly changed the subject. Although he denied feelings of depression or anger, his responses on the Rorschach suggested strong feelings of both sadness and anger.

The most telling moment came on a test where he had to take a series of scrambled pictures, like the cells of a comic strip, and arrange them in a sequence telling a story. Used in the standard way, this is a test of logical reasoning and social awareness. Matthew did fine on the first five of these tasks. On the sixth, he was handed a series of pictures that showed an encounter between two men where, in one of the cells, one punches the other. Upon seeing these pictures, he immediately picked up the card depicting the punch, put it between his teeth, bit it in half, and threw the two pieces on the floor. He then took the remaining cards and put them in order making up a story excluding the one he had broken.

Without saying anything, Matthew told me everything. There was violence going on in his home. He had to live the story of his life without including this information, yet everything in his life had changed because of it. The story-telling task circumvented his defenses in a way that allowed him to communicate with me without violating the promise of silence he had made to his mother's boyfriend. His abuse was later verified in family therapy, as were his mother's difficulties in parenting and knowing how to protect Matthew and herself from abuse. Matthew slowly healed after the boyfriend was removed from the home and both he and his mother received therapy.

Silence as a Background for Communication

One of the primary ways that psychotherapy violates the rules of normal social interactions is through the acceptance and uses of silence. Silence is powerfully evocative of projective processes and may be the ultimate blank screen. In silence, we can imagine being in the arms of someone who loves and accepts us, or stand in humiliation and be the object of contempt. Silences can evoke powerful emotions from our clients' memories, but the client will not necessarily remember the historical context in which they were formed. Because you are in the room with the client, he or she will assume you are the one evoking them. This is the projective process of transference.

Silence is especially powerful because we experience so little of it in the modern world. Being silent in the presence of another is often "awkward" and usually means that something is wrong with us or the relationship. Thus, silence is equated with shame and incompetence, both of which evoke anxiety. In some cultures, sitting in silence with others for hours is not unusual, nor does it evoke discomfort. So ask yourself: "What does silence evoke for my client as well as me?" Given the opportunity, each client will teach you what silence means to him or her. In so doing, clients will also provide you with information about the architecture of their unconscious world.

Silence can be experienced as safety, acceptance, indifference, abandonment, or damnation. I have had clients, furious at me for not filling the silence, say such things as "What the hell am I paying you for, to sit there like a jerk and not say anything?" Other clients have praised me for the very same behavior: "You are the first person who has given me the time to think through my answer. My husband gets so impatient with me that he just walks away," or "My father would yell at me to answer him and I would only get more paralyzed and mute," or "Thank you for letting me be here without either of us having to say a thing." Some clients are unable to tolerate silence, and, in truth, neither can some therapists. If this is the case with you, it is important to discover if it is the client's discomfort or your own discomfort that leads you to fill the silence. You may be retreating from something that is potentially beneficial for your client.

We can all become uncomfortable with silence, client and therapist alike, because of our social conditioning and personal history. Therapists often feel pressure to speak, feeling like they need to be "doing something" because simply "being" with the client is enough. When you listen to tapes of your sessions, see if you tend to fill silences. If you do, consider allowing the silences to go past your level of comfort and explore your feelings and associations. What do you feel? What makes you anxious about the silence? What does silence mean in your family of origin? Do any of the following statements reflect your own inner thoughts?

If I am silent:

- My client will think I'm incompetent.
- My client will go crazy or lose control.
- I will go crazy or lose control.
- My client won't like me.
- My client will think I'm stupid.
- I'm a bad therapist.
- I feel like I'll just scream!

When I question students about the lack of silence during a session, they most often begin by saying that they fill silences to relax their clients. After reflection, they usually realize that they fill silence just as much to soothe themselves. Ten or fifteen seconds of silence may feel like an eternity in social situations but should not be unusual in therapy. Silence is an important aspect of therapeutic communication, something to be seriously considered and fully explored.

If you have trouble estimating time during silences, try this technique. Set up a clock with a sweep second hand somewhere behind the client. Put it in a place that you can see easily with a glance. Pay attention to how long you allow silences to continue and, if 5 or 10 seconds seems long to you, let the silence stretch out to 15, 30, or even a minute as you grow more comfortable. If you find that silences go on for a minute or two, you might want to ask your client gently, "Are you aware that you are silent?" or "What are you feeling?" to regain verbal contact. Each client will have a different period of silence tolerance. For some, silence will be helpful, whereas for others it may feel like abandonment. If this is the case with a particular client, you may chose to start by carrying the conversation for a short time and gradually shift responsibility to the client.

In order to utilize silence in a positive way, we have to help our clients become comfortable with it. Before this can happen, we have to become comfortable with silence ourselves. Notice the role of silence in your everyday life and experiment with longer and deeper periods of silence. If you tend to avoid silence, experiment with increasing the amount of silence you can tolerate and pay close attention to the thoughts and feelings that emerge. Yoga and meditation classes can help, as well as readings that are designed to increase self-awareness.

Within the therapy relationship, silence provides a space for shared contemplation and mutual acceptance. Neither you nor your client needs to be charming, entertaining, or witty. Take the performance pressure off of both of you and try to create a context for self-reflection and mutual discovery. Sometimes the best strategy is no strategy at all.

CHAPTER SEVEN

The Therapist's Feelings
Anticipated
and Unanticipated

> When you do not know your personal devil, he usually manifests himself in the nearest person.
> —PAULO COELHO

AS BEGINNING THERAPISTS, we usually think of therapy as something we do *to* a client, like a doctor setting a bone or a teacher correcting a wrong answer. In reality, therapy is a process that we do *with* a client. We soon come to experience a wide range of pleasant and not-so-pleasant feelings as we enter into our clients' challenges and struggles. I certainly didn't anticipate experiencing so many feelings before I began to see clients. I thought being "professional" meant putting your own feelings aside, and what I understood of taking a neutral stance only reinforced my notion of the emotionless therapist. It took time for me to realize that, although I had to make a decision about what emotions to show, I needed to be keenly aware of my feelings and use them in my work.

Before I began to practice psychotherapy, I did anticipate feelings of excitement and satisfaction. I imagined my future clients struggling through powerful internal conflicts that would feed my need for a steady diet of exciting and life-changing insights. Clients would show their appreciation by sending their friends to see me, my reputation would spread, and my practice would boom. Being a therapist might be emotionally draining at times, but each session would culminate in a burst of insight and personal growth.

Imagine my surprise when I actually started seeing clients! Where did all this ambivalence and resistance come from? What happened to the rapid enlightenment and profuse gratitude? I never anticipated clients' being angry with me or sleepless nights wondering if I had done the right thing. My first thought was that I had chosen the wrong career. Over time, I realized that the day-to-day life of a therapist was far different than my fantasies.

Impatience

Prior to seeing clients, I had little idea of the power of resistance. I thought that once I was a therapist, clients would accept my assistance and follow my suggestions. The thought of struggling with my impatience with a client's progress never occurred to me. Although some clients do benefit from short-term therapy many, especially those who have deep-seated characterological problems, take years to show improvement. Some clients progress on pace with what feels like geological time.

Resistance has been referred to as "paradoxical reluctance." People come to you at considerable expense of time and money, and then proceed to resist your help. What sense does this make? Why recognize that things need to change, make a commitment to changing, seek assistance to change, and then insist on not changing? This familiar scenario can only make sense in light of the unconscious. With most clients, the biggest challenge isn't finding a helpful diagnosis or establishing a good treatment plan, it is helping them to become open to change.

Every therapist desires to feel effective, important, and successful. It is easy to feel thwarted by difficult clients who have complex problems and lack good social skills. We often receive the brunt of their criticism, and they may use their lack of progress to attack our knowledge and skills. The term "blaming the victim" was originally used to refer to groups within society who suffer economic and social discrimination while being simultaneously blamed for their lack of success. In the same way, we can blame the client for their lack of progress to protect ourselves from our own feelings of failure.

Labeling a client as resistant or pathological can be motivated by anger from our hurt feelings, frustration for not being able to solve their problems, or revenge for making us feel incompetent. This kind of countertransference-based diagnosis can take many forms. For example, it is easier to label hostile clients as "borderline" than it is to consider the possibility that some of their complaints may be legitimate. We can accuse clients of not wanting to get better in order to manipulate those around them and give them a more severe diagnosis to justify our therapeutic impotence. Ask yourself if the labels you are using with your clients are truly helping you to help them.

Having said all this, cases of court-ordered treatment (or when clients are compensated for disabilities) create situations where clients may be motivated to stay ill. The same goes for clients who gain the attention and help of others because of their symptoms. Keep in mind that a lack of progress can occur for many reasons.

I've gradually come to accept the varied and sometimes slow pace of therapy. Slow progress is actually the norm, and periods of "backsliding" should be expected. It is important, especially when progress is slow and difficult, to have a good case conceptualization and revisit it on a regular basis. We all need to be reminded of what we are doing and why. Use difficulties in the therapy as opportunities to rethink your treatment strategies and get consultation from other professionals. When you recognize stagnation in the therapy, it is time to become curious, ask questions, and seek answers.

"Hey, That Was My Insight!"

Many clients grow up in families where it is dangerous to accept assistance or advice. Children betrayed by their parents or their parents' bad judgment tend to grow into adults without the concept that others can be helpful. They are skeptical of your knowledge and suspicious of your motives and intentions. These clients often reflexively reject your ideas, interpretations, and concerns. This is a common manifestation of transference. As a result, establishing a trusting therapeutic relationship can take a long time and involve many tests of your competence and trustworthiness.

I have been in many situations where a client is beginning to share some recently discovered insight. I wait in anticipation, only to hear something I suggested weeks or months ago. When I suggested the same thing back then, it was either ignored or dismissed as silly. I remember early in my career having thoughts like "Hey, I told you that a few weeks ago and you just rolled your eyes at me! Now you tell me it's your idea as if I never said a thing about it! Give me some credit!"

I realized that this reaction was childish even as I experienced it. Yet, I was struggling to feel competent and it was hard to not receive the credit I thought I deserved. I have since learned to accept these feelings and gain reassurance in other ways. What works best in such situations is to be happy for the client and pay attention to a pattern of this type of behavior. If you eventually move to working on issues of trust and depending on others, you can use carefully chosen examples of these types of interactions to initiate discussion. Try saying something like "I've noticed on a number of occasions you have rejected some of my thoughts only to bring them back later as good ideas. I was wondering if you are aware of this and, if you are, can you tell me what thoughts or feelings you have about it."

If the client is able to understand and discuss the process, you might follow with something like, "You said that your father was always giving you advice that you felt wasn't right for you. Could you be protecting yourself from me like you had to from him?" In this way, you can connect something that is happening in the therapeutic relationship with the client's history and unconscious emotional world. This is an example of a transference interpretation. Remember, though, that the therapeutic relationship needs to be strong and sustained in order to delve into these deeper issues.

Another variant of this dynamic occurs when clients find it impossible to work through difficult topics during sessions. They may change the subject or tell you they will "work on it" later. They take in what you say like a shoplifter, sliding it under their jacket, waiting to get away from your gaze and examine it when they feel safe. This is a pattern that gets established in childhood and becomes a salient aspect of all their relationships. Many clients fear that if they reveal what they think and feel, it will be taken away, modified, or invalidated. Having parents who always told them what they *should* think and feel taught them that transparency and collaboration are dangerous.

When clients have grown up with parents who are mentally ill, addicted to substances, narcissistic, or competitive with them, they may learn that parental advice and counsel was incorrect or even destructive. Bright children in these situations learn not to depend on others. Why would individuals who needed protection from their own parents take your competence and good intentions for granted? They will keep their needs secret, and try, as best they can, to nurture, soothe, and support themselves in private. It is important to remember that this form of transference must be respected and approached with caution. Interpreting these adaptive defenses too quickly runs the risk of overwhelming your client and possibly driving them to terminate therapy prematurely.

Sexual Attraction

The prohibition against physical intimacy creates a boundary that protects both client and therapist from harm. It also provides a context for the therapeutic work that would be impossible in the absence of this boundary. Yet that boundary, like any taboo, generates tension. Often unanticipated by new therapists, sexual attraction is quite common in the therapy relationship. The emotional intimacy of therapy can naturally lead to a longing for physical closeness.

It is almost impossible to see a movie portrayal of a psychotherapist who doesn't become sexually involved with his or her client. Of course, sex sells movie tickets, but this depiction of therapists also reflects a real problem in our field. Despite increased awareness and added focus during training, the phenomenon continues, as do the ranks of therapists who damage their clients and careers. Although our usual response to warnings against sexual involvement with clients is "I know better than that," no therapist is immune to boundary violations with clients. This fact was made clear to me when I discovered that one of my ethics professors lost her license in this way.

Although it is difficult to discuss sexual attraction to a client, it is vital to do so. Jill, a brave student in my group supervision, raised her hand and asked if she could discuss a client she was seeing. Anxious and frightened, Jill hesitantly told of her dilemma. She was seeing a male client, one of her first, who was about her age. As she described his problems and the course of treatment, she mentioned a number of times how attractive he was. From the way she talked about him, it was clear that she had feelings for him that went beyond their professional relationship.

Her client had a history of chaotic relationships, a past suicide attempt, and severe mood swings. He had worked with many different therapists, and he told Jill that she was the best therapist he had ever had—perhaps "the best therapist ever." She felt they had developed a strong emotional bond and that he was benefiting from treatment. The reason she wanted to discuss this case was because the client had suggested they become lovers.

Jill had taken classes for years and had heard all of the theoretical discussions about borderline pathology, sexualized transference, and the parameters of the therapeutic relationship. Because I knew all of this, I expected her to ask about specific strategies and techniques for dealing with her client's sexualized transference. To my surprise, she asked the group, "Do you think that having a romantic relationship with him is a good idea given our therapeutic relationship?" At first, I thought I misunderstood and looked to others in the supervision group to see if I had heard correctly. They all looked back at me, flabbergasted. I took a moment to catch my breath, turned back to Jill, and asked her to repeat her question. We had all heard correctly.

Jill was enamored of her client. She was single, worked too hard, and did not have satisfying personal relationships. Because of her own emptiness and intense need for intimacy, it was difficult for her to see this client's attraction as transference. She also lost track of the context of his seductive behavior; he had a history of early sexual abuse as well as a personality disorder. Her heart was captured by the physical attraction, and she was soothed by his praise of her therapeutic abilities and felt rescued from her feelings of isolation when in his presence.

Jill's own history of sexual and physical abuse—and all the boundary violations she had experienced—made a dual relationship with her client seem familiar. Jill forgot her professional training as she regressed into the emotional world of her early family relationships. She admitted that she had begun to fantasize about a future with this client, and had a vague sense that they would have to eventually discontinue their therapeutic relationship.

I was as impressed with Jill's honesty as I was with her ability to completely ignore so much of what she had learned. Such is the power of dissociation, repression, and denial. In reality, what she had learned was still there; it was urging her to make her inner struggle public so she might break out of her unconscious trance. I could see that the other students were aghast at her disclosure, so I made a point of normalizing her feelings and praising her courage. We discussed the case in great detail and I predicted that if she held to the therapeutic boundaries and strategies, she could be successful with this attractive and seductive client.

In a matter of weeks, her client's positive transference shifted to its negative counterpart, and she became the worst therapist he had ever known. He was enraged that she rebuffed his seductions, and he spent many sessions berating her skills. Over time, however, she was able to do some important work with him and helped him to be able to discuss his feelings instead of acting them out in their relationship.

Initially, Jill had only seen the positive side of her client's borderline splitting and was seduced by his ability to find and exploit her weaknesses. In retrospect, she was extremely thankful that she had discussed the case and maintained appropriate therapeutic boundaries. Now that she had seen this side of his personality disorder, it was difficult for her to imagine her fantasies of a future with him. I was grateful that she was able to weather this storm without making a mistake that could have sabotaged her career. By becoming a therapist, Jill had hoped to put her painful past behind her, only to find that it was once again causing her pain and confusion and risking her well-being. This experience highlighted Jill's fragile ego and vulnerability to regress with certain clients. She realized that she had dodged a bullet aimed at both her heart and career, and it became clear that she needed to be in therapy herself.

Sex should never be a part of any therapy relationship. It is not in the best interest of your client no matter how compelling it may be for you. For those of you who have difficulty maintaining boundaries for the benefit of your client, it may help to keep the following in mind: If you are physically intimate with a client, you are giving him or her the power to end your career. Think about all of the work, energy, and money you have invested in your training. Ask yourself if this is the kind of power you want to give to a client. If you are seriously considering giving in to your sexual attraction for a client, call a colleague, your supervisor, or your therapist as soon as possible. Think it out, work it out, but *never* act it out!

The Power of Regression

Regression is the activation of powerful early emotional memories that bring us back to previous times in our lives. Regression is similar to the experience of flashbacks in that it activates many of the same neural networks of unconscious memory, superimposing past emotional dramas onto the present. Jill's experience with her client in the previous section is a good example of regression in a therapist that is unhelpful to the therapeutic process.

Regression can be important for a client, however, because it activates old networks of memory that can be key to the development of symptoms. The enhancement of regression was one of Freud's goals in having his client lie down, face away from him, and spend time in silence. Encouraging clients to talk about their past, supporting the expression of strong feelings, and drawing parallels between therapy and parenting all enhance regression. They diminish attention to the present and allow the mind to drift backward through subjective time.

Although I had always heard that therapy could be a powerful trigger for regressive experiences, I was surely convinced the first time I experienced it myself. During one particularly painful session in my own therapy, I revisited a very difficult time in my childhood. My parents' relationship was disintegrating, the family was in financial peril, and I had no one I could talk to about my own terror. I experienced many strong and painful emotions as I relived these memories.

Some of the dissociative defenses I employed during childhood became manifest, and I had difficulty staying oriented as an adult in therapy. After the session, I went back to my car and found that I had no idea how to drive! I sat in the car, more than a little scared, wondering what to do. Fortunately, the memory of driving slowly emerged as my childhood memories receded. My understanding of what happened to me was that the power of those early experiences eclipsed my present reality and I "regressed" to an earlier set of emotions, knowledge, and self-identity.

Another example of regression comes from a client who had a repetitive dream about entering the home of her grandparents. The dream always began by her entering the house through the front door into a foyer with a mirror that faced the entry. She would see herself in the mirror and turn to the left to go into the living room. As she went further back into her memories of childhood and more primitive emotions emerged, she noticed that these dreams began to change. What she first noticed was that when she entered the house she no longer saw her image in the mirror. At first, she thought the mirror was gone, but she then to realized that she was now having the same dream as a much younger child and was no longer tall enough to look into it.

Therapists need to have a great deal of respect for the power of regression, both for their clients and themselves. The student considering an affair with her client found herself with someone who wanted to bring sexuality into a relationship in which it could only play a destructive role. This paralleled her childhood experiences so closely that she regressed from a confident adult to a confused and dependent child. The power of regression allowed her to consider violating therapeutic boundaries despite her training. It is absolutely necessary for therapists to be courageous in the exploration of their own internal worlds and ever-vigilant to networks of unconscious memory that become activated during our work.

Doctor Heal Thyself

Over the years, I have had a number of clients of whom I was jealous. They have had beautiful spouses, children, and homes, and successful, lucrative careers. A number of my clients have been more psychologically healthy than I. These realizations are humbling and sometimes confusing when we are in the role of healer. They can also trigger our personal struggles with imperfection and shame.

The road to being a therapist has many twists and turns. I have been surprised by both the number and depth of the personal issues I have had to confront over the years. From childhood, I had developed the ability to hide many of my own problems from myself by focusing on helping others. As long as I was distracted by attending to others, I felt pretty good. In the absence of distraction I became vulnerable to the spontaneous experience of my own feelings and became anxious and sad. The journey inward though my own emotional world has been as important to my ability to be a therapist as everything I learned in school about the psyche and therapeutic techniques. I have also come to find that this learning is a lifelong process that will continue until my last breath.

I have also had to struggle with the fact that, like me, many people in the field of mental health have their own psychological difficulties; in fact, this may be a primary (unconscious) reason they are in the field. Put a group of us together in a facility designed to help clients and you find that at least half of our time and attention is dedicated to taking care of each other. For years, I found this confusing and demoralizing, and I wondered why we couldn't put our own problems aside and just do our jobs? After much reflection, I realized that this attitude doesn't work. Everyone in mental health, clients and caretakers alike, needs help, support, and healing. Trying to help clients without helping the helpers ultimately fails.

Once I was walking down the hall of a psychiatric ward and having a discussion with one of my clients. He was a soft-spoken, well-educated man who had recently suffered an acute psychotic episode. As we walked, we passed the closed door of the ward chief, who was screaming uncontrollably at one of the nurses. From what we could hear, it sounded very much like the incoherent ramblings of a new client before being sedated. As we continued on our way, my client, in a calm and philosophical way, stated, "It's often hard for me to tell the doctors from the clients. Good thing we're all locked up."

As I shifted my expectations, I discovered that I also needed the help I was giving to others on the staff and began gradually taking it. Striking a balance between all of these needs was an important turning point in my ability to work with both clients and groups of mental health workers. I've learned to be more honest and realistic about my own needs for support. My investment in coworkers is no longer a distraction from my job but rather an essential aspect of my contribution to all of our clients.

CHAPTER EIGHT

It's Scary to Go to Therapy
The Paradox
of Client Resistance

> I had a lot to learn before I could figure out
> how much I had to learn.
>
> —A SUCCESSFUL CLIENT

ONE OF THE MOST DIFFICULT aspects of being a new therapist is learning how to deal with client resistance. Most of us make the mistake of thinking that resistance is like a rain delay—something to wait through before we can get started. Nothing could be further from the truth. Working with and working through resistance are key therapeutic skills. Many of the answers to a client's difficulties are woven into the resistance he or she brings into the therapy relationship. With time, we gradually learn to decipher the important information embedded within resistance.

Beginning therapists often first identify resistance in the content of what a client says. *Content resistance* is reflected in emotional difficulties around certain topics. Strong emotions or gaps in the discussion are often the first indications that "something is going on in there." A client may always look sad when he mentions his sister, another may talk a great deal about her father but never mention her mother. Sometimes a client will say, "I don't want to talk about that," and go on to another topic. These are all examples of content resistance.

With increased experience, therapists begin to recognize what is called *process resistance*. Process resistance is embedded in personality, coping styles, and defenses formed during development. Our brains are shaped through adaptation to experiences and, in turn, organize our adult perceptions in line with what has come before. In this way the past becomes the present and future, or, put another way, we create what we expect to find. A prime example of this is the transference relationship, through which the client experiences the therapist as a significant person (or persons) from the past.

New therapists often get their first view of process resistance in situations of setting and collecting fees, missed appointments, and early termination. These are arenas in which a client will "act out" his or her resistance. It is up to the therapist to understand and name the acting out, as well as discover the underlying emotional processes motivating the behaviors. It is particularly difficult for beginners to confront these situations, and it takes time to gain the confidence needed to overcome the discomfort of making process interpretations. It is easier to avoid discussing missed sessions or bad checks than to have frank discussions about the thoughts and feelings motivating them.

It is scary to go to therapy, and ambivalence is the norm. Just making the decision to go can be nerve-wracking, let alone making the appointment and sitting in the waiting room anticipating the therapist's arrival. Wild and unfettered enthusiasm is often a well-practiced form of resistance. By the time I walked into my first session, I was a giddy mess. The voices in my head kept telling me things like "the therapist will think I'm crazy," or "he'll think my parents did a bad job," or, worst of all, "he'll tell me I'm too screwed up to be a therapist." Remembering these experiences helps me to be more empathic with new clients.

In light of all of these concerns and fears, it is important to do what you can to make clients more comfortable. Begin by complimenting them on their decision to seek help, then guide them though the early sessions. If they have difficulty beginning, start off with some general and nonthreatening questions, such as asking about their education, interests, and hobbies. Get a sense of your clients as people and don't start out with both feet in your abnormal psychology textbook.

Not only is it scary to go to therapy, but it can also be scary to confront clients on their defenses and resistances. Given our standard roles as peacekeepers in our families, many therapists do anything they can to avoid conflict. This may be especially true for women, given the expectation in most cultures that the role of a woman is to take care of others and make them feel better. Countless female students, clients, and friends have told me that if they say or do anything that upsets anyone they feel like they are being a "bitch." It is certainly important to be able to distinguish between being a bitch and making a valid interpretation.

Many therapists were not allowed to express anger in their childhoods. The dynamics of their families and the needs of others required them to be the good girl or boy. The problem with not being allowed to be angry during development is that it does not get integrated into daily life and normal interactions.

Because of this, when anger is expressed, it is explosive, frightening, and serves as further evidence that it needs to be suppressed. Unfortunately, when anger is deleted from conscious experience, power and appropriate assertiveness usually get lost as well.

Although certainly not the goal of therapy, conflict is sometimes important for growth. We need to be able to face our clients' anger and absorb negative transference despite our discomfort with being the target of these feelings. Remember that below many a positive transference lurks negative transference; resistance implies a defense against something that is provoking anxiety. Whereas some people hide their anger with a smile, others keep their vulnerability hidden behind a shield of rage.

A therapist's fear of confrontation may be indicated by some of the following untherapeutic behaviors:

- Not discussing multiple time changes for appointments
- Avoiding discussion of missed sessions or lateness for sessions
- Avoiding discussion concerning the collection of fees
- Setting fees too low
- Not bringing up difficult topics
- Not making interpretations or making too many interpretations
- Cutting sessions short or running overtime
- Missing sessions

Make a point of exploring your relationship to anger, assertiveness, and power in your personal therapy, and pay special attention to the therapeutic issues just described.

The Basic Paradox

At first it is confusing: A client comes to therapy, often at great emotional and financial expense, only to ward off your assistance, suggestions, and interpretations. Resistance is the basic paradox of psychotherapy, but only on the psychic *surface*. As you become familiar with a client's history, family, and the emotional challenges faced during development, his or her form of resistance will make more and more sense. Resistance is a form of implicit memory, an adaptation to the past that reverberates in the present. As you gain experience, you will learn to spot it during the first few minutes of interacting with a new client.

Clients' core issues are embedded within their resistances. I have had a number of clients who were severely abused by their fathers when they were young boys. Jason, a 29-year-old baseball player, spent the first session with his arms defiantly folded across his chest, daring me to make him feel anything. Doug, a middle-aged business consultant, brought me gifts nearly every session. Tony, a teenager three times my size, pushed his chair back into the corner of my office and looked as if he expected me to attack him. Each of these men had made many unconscious adaptations to their early abuse and were demonstrating them to me in the transference relationship. Although all three clearly remembered being abused, none was aware how his adaptation had become interwoven into his personality, defenses, and interpersonal behaviors.

Sometimes, symptoms work to provide us with something we need that we are unable to ask for directly. A husband who can't get his needs met may be taken care of when he is sick, or an overworked mother who develops panic attacks and agoraphobia discovers that her family begins to share some of her burden. An adolescent, nervous about leaving his depressed mother, finds that his increasing symptoms of anxiety are an acceptable reason to postpone leaving for college. Rewards, or negative things that get to be avoided because of symptoms, are called *secondary gains*. These benefits serve to reinforce and maintain symptoms, making clients more resistant to change.

The key to dealing with secondary gains is to help clients attain the things they need directly. Assisting clients in identifying needs and being more assertive about attaining them is almost always helpful. In other cases, such as with the adolescent with the depressed mother, getting his mother the help she needs takes him off the hook, allowing him to stay on a healthier developmental course. When people have their needs met directly, they are less likely to hold on to the self-damaging symptoms they use to get them.

What we call "resistance" is a necessary form of communication from client to therapist and a central component of the therapeutic process. Although the word *resistance* is commonly used in psychotherapy, it is still uncertain whether the term is appropriate. What we are discussing may be better described as implicit and procedural memories from early relationships or traumatic experiences. Although outside of conscious awareness, these memories heavily influence how people experience the world and the ways in which they respond to it.

Although clients are often aware that they are engaging in repetitive patterns, few understand their origin in unconscious memory. One key role of the therapist is to identify, understand, and communicate these patterns to the client.

We try to educate clients about how their past reverberates in the present and shapes the future. Describing it as a form of memory helps to avoid blaming clients or establishing an adversarial relationship. It is far better to think in terms of a collaboration, where there is a mutual exploration of how the client's brain has learned to adapt and survive.

Meeting Resistance with Acceptance

Aikido is a style of marital arts based on principles of balance and energy. The core philosophy of Aikido is that if someone is attacking you, he must be mentally unbalanced. In this context, the role of the Aikidoist is to protect the attacker from his bad judgment until his balance can be restored. Therefore, the power of the attacker is not confronted head-on with oppositional power but avoided with a skillful side-step. The energy of the attack is then channeled into a circular movement that evolves into a nondestructive hold. When a move is executed correctly, neither the attacked nor the attacker are injured.

The way of Aikido is a wonderful metaphor for confronting resistance in psychotherapy. The biggest risk for a new therapist is to take the client's resistance personally and meet it with his or her own ego-driven energy. As in Aikido, resistance is an indication that the client needs assistance in attaining psychic balance and integration. Although it is entirely natural to have an emotional reaction to your clients' resistance, remaining centered and mindful of your therapeutic role is essential. Retaliation, although often tempting, is almost certainly the wrong thing to do. Resistance needs to be acknowledged, understood, and appreciated if it is to be successfully converted into an acceptance of new ways of thinking, feeling, and being. Acceptance of the client's resistance as a necessary defense in light of past challenges is a central aspect of therapeutic success.

Over the course of your career, you will be faced with a hundred forms of resistance; the question is how you deal with them. The first rule, which may be the most difficult to follow, is: *Don't be defensive.* Remember that the resistance is probably about the client and not about you. Second, listen carefully to the client's concerns. There may, in fact, be realistic aspects to their concerns about your skills or knowledge that should be thought through and discussed before proceeding. For example, a client may realize that he is difficult and in need of an experienced therapist rather than a beginning one. Some clients may have issues that are too embarrassing to discuss with a therapist of the opposite sex. After listening to a client's concerns, ask yourself: *How might the client be right?* A client's questions give you another opportunity to not know; after all, none of us can guarantee that we can help every client we see.

Think about the following questions:

- Do I have the skills to treat this client?
- Are we a good match?
- Might this client benefit more from working with another therapist?
- Do I feel that I can help this client?
- Am I having a strong countertransference reaction that may compromise my ability to help this particular client?

These are difficult and complicated questions to answer. It takes years to gain the necessary experience to come to good decisions, so rely on your supervisor's help while you can.

If you have seriously considered a client's objections and engaged in your own self-reflection and it still seems more like resistance than a legitimate concern, move on to the next step: Try to make sense of why your client needs his or her resistance. Explore the client's relationship history and the quality and degree of support he or she has received from others. As discussed in the last chapter, it may be that the client has been betrayed or misled by those he or she depended upon most. The resistance may be based on previous experiences with doctors or other mental health practitioners. I have had several clients who have been victims of therapist malpractice; the first phase of treatment was entirely focused on issues of my own competence and trustworthiness. On a more benign level, it may be that you remind a client of a car salesman who once sold them a lemon. The point is, resistance has been learned from experience for the purpose of survival in some other context. It needs to be accepted, discovered, and explored and not taken personally.

Although the underlying motivation for resistance is usually not about the therapist, it is often framed in the context of therapist attributes, behaviors, or shortcomings. Have you been told by clients that you are too young or old, too white or black, too gay or straight to understand or be of any help? Clients may look at you suspiciously and ask, "How many cases have you had?" or "How many years have you been a therapist?" or even "Did you at least go to an accredited school?" Of course, the less experience you have or the less impressive your credentials, the more impact these thinly disguised attacks may have on your ego and equilibrium.

When your personal attributes, credentials, or abilities are questioned, it is natural to become defensive and angry. Of course, these negative emotions are detrimental to both the client's view of you and the therapeutic relationship. The best strategy is to be prepared to have your skills and abilities questioned so you can respond in a confident and nondefensive manner. Try responses such as "I'm just beginning my training as a therapist. I chose to work at this clinic because of the reputation of the supervision. As you know, I am under the supervision of a licensed therapist and we review each session together."

It is the client's right to know about your training and experience, and having them questioned or even challenged is not necessarily an indication of resistance. However, pay attention to how clients ask you about your qualifications. If their questions are asked in the emotional context of sarcasm, condescension, or anger, they may represent important information about the client's expectations, past experiences, or defenses. If this is the case, you may want to follow a direct answer about the quality of your training with a question such as "Are you hopeful about being helped by therapy?" or "How do you feel it will be to work together?" Questions such as these may get directly to their fears and concerns about entering therapy.

I have had clients tell me that I have no right to treat someone with schizophrenia because I've never experienced it, or that I don't know what depression is because I have a "perfect life." I've also been told that I couldn't possibly understand an adolescent growing up today because I grew up in a time before peer pressure and drugs. Simple phrases like "teach me" or "you're right, I don't understand what you are going through but I would like to learn," can disarm initial resistance and help establish a healthy therapeutic relationship.

What a client is usually asking through criticisms, challenges, and attacks is "Can you help me?" or "Can I trust you?" This is where I try to guide the discussion when I'm challenged. In conversations about my age, gender, race, or training, my underlying message is "I don't know if I can help you, but I'd like to try." Do I need to be of the same religion, experience the same prejudices, or have the same illness as clients in order to help them? Can they teach me about what their world is like and help me to help them? Would they be better off with a gay, black, or Jewish therapist? Perhaps they would, but in the course of these discussions, we usually establish a relationship that evolves into psychotherapy.

Keep some of these principles in mind when you encounter resistance:

- Don't take it personally and never retaliate.
- Don't punish your clients for their resistance (e.g., "So you think I'm a lousy therapist; well, you're a pretty shitty client!").
- Accept it, validate it, and give your clients credit for using their defenses when they were necessary (e.g., "You were absolutely right to not show your weaknesses to your parents because they *did* use them against you.").
- Explore it as you would any other unconscious memory.
- Give clients words for their resistance so they can come to recognize and understand it (e.g., "It seems that you become quiet and withdrawn whenever you feel criticized. Next time you are withdrawing, see if you can notice it and even try to tell me when it is happening.").

- Contextualize it. Discuss when it was necessary in the past and distinguish the past from the present.
- Set up situations where the client can experiment with not resisting (e.g., "Instead of canceling your appointment when you are feeling frightened, why not call, tell me you are frightened, and come to your appointment *with* your fear.").
- Most important: Be patient. Today's resistance contains tomorrow's insights.

Dealing With Cancellations

Therapists commonly react to cancellations with feelings of annoyance, anger, fear, or rejection. When clients call to cancel, it is easy to feel devalued and marginalized; we may feel we are not important enough to them to be a priority. These relatively common situations can evoke our own feelings of rejection, abandonment, and shame. We may also worry about what our supervisors will think or, later, in private practice, we can be angry about the negative financial impact of cancellations.

I have had many beginning therapists report that when a client cancels, their first assumption is that the client has decided they are incompetent. The cancellation activates their shame and they secretly feel the client has made the right choice in abandoning them. In cases like this, it is easy to see how difficult it is to do therapy when our own shame is so easily triggered; the cancellation becomes about us and not the client's defenses.

I had a client named Joseph who called to cancel nearly every appointment days, hours, or minutes before the session.

At first, my primary experience was annoyance; I set up my day to see clients at certain times and these constant cancellations felt disrespectful and almost abusive. I felt that Joseph devalued me, the therapy, and my time. As my attunement to Joseph's internal world deepened, I learned that his cancellations served a variety of needs. They provided him a lifeline to me between sessions, a way to act out how painful his life felt, and an opportunity to exercise his power and feel a sense of control—although *he* had chosen to come to therapy, he still felt I controlled him.

This same pattern played out on a regular basis in his personal relationships; he would withdraw from others at the slightest possibility of failure or rejection. As I continued to translate his cancellations into his needs for contact and control, he was more and more able to come in and discuss his needs rather than acting them out. During this process, the number of canceled sessions decreased and I invited Joseph to leave me a message whenever he felt he needed contact.

A client calling to cancel an appointment can mean anything. People do get flat tires, find themselves stuck in traffic, and run overtime in business meetings. But more often than not, cancellations are a client's way of telling you something. Based on what you have learned about the client, try to translate cancellations into their emotional meaning. Ask yourself what the client gains or avoids by canceling. How does it fit into his or her defenses, history, and presenting problems?

Many clients are afraid of becoming dependent on you or having you see that they are in pain and need help. In an effort to avoid being dependent, they might cancel because they feel too safe and comfortable. The fact that you are doing a good job and providing them with a trusting and caring relationship may lead them to cancel sessions and resist treatment. If a client has repeatedly experienced feeling hope at the beginning of relationships only to be let down or abandoned later, feelings of hope in therapy may trigger anxiety because of the expectation of the rejection to follow. Some of us learn to do unto others before they do unto us.

Consider these ideas when trying to understand why a client might cancel an appointment:

- Were any uncomfortable (or potentially uncomfortable) topics discussed during the previous session?
- Does the client seem to be getting *less* comfortable in therapy?
- Does the client seem to be getting *more* comfortable in therapy?
- Is the client becoming dependent on you?
- What was your frame of mind during the last session? Were you as present as usual or were you distracted, upset, or having any feelings that may have affected your work?
- How has the client left relationships in the past? Could this missed session be a prelude to termination?

Premature Termination

Premature termination is a common problem in psychotherapy. Clients discontinue for a variety of reasons. If a client isn't ready for therapy he or she will not stay, and no amount of skill will keep him or her in treatment. Some clients come in, take a look, and never come back. Rather than thinking in terms of preventing all premature terminations, learn to retain clients who are ready for therapy.

Clients who have been in therapy for just a few months rarely come in and say, "You know, I've been thinking of terminating and want to discuss these feelings with you." More commonly, they will leave a message informing you of their decision to terminate, having already made up their minds. If a client is terminating because the therapy is upsetting his or her psychic equilibrium, discussing the situation in an open manner may be difficult; the client may have to stick to the decision to maintain a sense of control. The very success of therapy will unsettle some clients and make them retreat to the safety of familiar defenses.

Because this is a common occurrence, during early sessions I ask clients about their relationship history and how they have left relationships in the past. Understanding what a client thinks and feels before leaving a relationship—and how he or she actually does it—reveals the person's defenses, coping strategies, and attachment patterns. It also provides you with a general idea of whether the client will terminate prematurely and how it may happen. The best strategy is to make clients aware of these patterns and have them alert you when they become activated.

Tom was an attractive 35-year-old executive who came to therapy complaining of anxiety and loneliness. In one of our first sessions I inquired about his past relationships—how they began, their course over time, and how they ended. As he described them, his relationships sounded somewhat superficial, based more on physical attraction and the roles he and his mates played in each others' lives than on emotional intimacy. He reported that in both of his significant relationships he gradually felt misunderstood, used, and unappreciated. He also said that there was no use in talking about it because his partners weren't capable of understanding him or taking care of his needs.

In both relationships, Tom moved out while his partner was away on business. They returned home to find that Tom and all his belongings were gone. Confused, each of the women contacted him in an attempt to understand what had happened. Tom reported that, in each instance, *he* was surprised that they were so surprised he was gone. He mused, "Couldn't they see that I was withdrawing from them over the last few weeks?"

My prediction was that during the course of treatment, my mistakes or empathic failures would be experienced but not named. He would accumulate a set of bad feelings, make decisions about my inadequacies, and then simply disappear. I brought up this idea and discussed it at some length during our third session. He thought it was an interesting hypothesis but couldn't imagine that I was correct. Tom assured me that because this was a therapeutic relationship and I was so attuned to him, he could never imagine terminating before he was done with therapy. Besides, he had many good reasons to leave his past relationships because of his partners' problems and I was nothing like those two women.

After 2 months of weekly sessions, Tom reported that something had changed; he started having stomach aches and bad dreams. He was certain that I was disappointed in his progress in therapy. I assured him that I wasn't having these feelings and that his physical symptoms and nightmares might be connected to feelings being evoked in our relationship. His father had been killed when he was a young child, and I felt that his feelings of closeness to me were activating emotional memories of his grief and loss. The bond developing between us may have triggered his withdrawal from caring for the fear that I might be someone he would lose.

Tom came in during the ninth week of treatment and shared with me his decision to terminate. When I suggested that we take some time to process these thoughts and feelings in case they were related to his pattern of abandonment, he sat quietly and stared at me. When I asked him what he was thinking, he responded with anger, "I get to choose my therapist!" He repeated this phrase a number of times as if he found it soothing to hear his own voice. Any attempt at discussion was experienced as manipulation and accompanied by anger. Tom had become rapidly overwhelmed; he felt he had to flee in order to protect himself from caring too much or getting too close. In this case, ours was just another failed relationship.

Fortunately, identifying patterns of relationship termination can help clients gain insight and avoid repeating them. What might have happened if Tom had shared his feelings of being misunderstood? We could have then tied his current reactions to therapy to the loss of his father and he could have become conscious of the transference of these feelings into *our* relationship. In the absence of an understanding of these processes, Tom was convinced that his feelings were a reaction to our relationship as opposed to a repetition of a painful drama from his past.

When thinking about a client's relationship history, pay attention to these basic points:

- Clarify and delineate the steps of the emotional and behavioral drama (describe the sequence of thoughts, feelings, and actions).
- Make the sequence of feelings and behaviors explicit.

- Remain vigilant for early signs of the withdrawal/termination process.
- Discuss the evidence with the client and (tentatively) predict what *may* happen next.
- Offer alternative strategies to acting out past patterns.
- Try to evoke memories of similar emotions in previous situations.

The therapeutic process can help break down repetitive patterns into stages of step-by-step thoughts and feelings. By becoming conscious of the various steps in these internal processes, the client increases his or her ability to notice and interrupt repetitive sequences. With clients who are ready, examining relationship patterns and predicting their activation can be useful tools for increasing insight and decreasing premature termination. It may take years and many repetitions of the pattern for clients to gain the perspective and maturity required to weather this kind of emotional storm.

Wanting to Fire a Client

It is not unusual for a therapist to fantasize about or find a way to "fire" a client. These urges take the form of forgetting important details about the client's life, hoping that he or she will call and cancel, or daydreams about referring him or her to another therapist. When this occurs, it makes sense to consider whether the client *should* be referred. Perhaps a particular client has problems that you are not trained to work with, your countertransference reaction is too strong, or you find that there is simply a personality conflict.

A strong countertransference reaction to a client could be a good reason to refer. Some clients remind us of problematic figures in our own lives or have symptoms that stir up a great deal of emotion within us. With good therapy and supervision, we can often turn countertransference reactions into personal growth and positive therapeutic experiences for our clients. At other times, strong countertransference reactions, especially at the beginning of treatment, may lead to a wise decision to refer.

There are many other reasons for referring a client to another therapist that are unrelated to countertransference. Some examples include:

- The client's psychological difficulties are beyond your level of training or supervision.
- The client suffers with symptoms that would be best helped by an expert in a specific therapy (e.g., a cognitive behaviorist who specializes in phobias or posttraumatic stress disorder).
- You discover some conflict of interest or dual relationship that could impede therapy (e.g., discovering that your client is married to your husband's boss).
- You and your supervisor come to genuinely believe that you are unable to help a particular client.

Clients who are ambivalent about or afraid of therapy may try to get you to fire them. They may be fearful that you will abandon them and try to gain power over this fear by forcing your hand. Clients may miss sessions, come early or late, bounce checks, come in drunk, or just sit for weeks and remain uninvolved in treatment. In these and countless other ways, they will try to precipitate the abandonment they so fear. Creating their own abandonment is a way to gain control over what they experience as a painful inevitability.

Clients who are aggressive, critical, yell at you, or spray you with sarcasm may seem to be begging to be referred or terminated. Their aggression may also be motivated by the expectation of aggression toward them. A client may have the unconscious strategy that a good offense is the best defense. Unfortunately, for many of these clients, this is a self-fulfilling prophesy that leaves them alone again and again. At a deeper level, they may be trying to make you feel their abandonment anxiety.

When a client seems to be begging to be terminated by treating you badly, ask yourself why. Why come to therapy for a fight? What is the significance of fighting for this client? Is it a form of contact, the only way he or she feels able to reach out to you and connect? This is often true for clients who have grown up feeling neglected, misunderstood, or abused. Anger may be the client's only bridge to people in his or her life.

A client's anger is often a reaction to a real need to depend on you and the fear that you will disappoint him or her. The very feeling generated in you—your anger and wanting to fire him or her—is the feeling the client needs you to withstand. It is a test of your centeredness, maturity, and availability. When you tolerate your feelings and identify the anger as a desire to connect, trust, and be loved, the anger is often converted to just that.

Discussing and Collecting Fees

One of my college friends often said, "Money is funny." At first, I thought this was just a silly rhyme, repeated in lieu of eloquence. It turns out he was right; money *is* funny. Though it is basic for our survival, we are supposed to act as if money isn't important. We are not supposed to talk about it or flaunt our wealth or success. We don't tell other people how much we earn and it is considered crude to mention what things cost. Disagreements about money can break up marriages, destroy friendships, and start wars. So, naturally, it is a difficult topic to confront in therapy.

Many clients come into therapy with the unconscious wish to be told that they will be seen for free. It seems so unfair to have to suffer at the hands of other people and then to have to pay to be cured. For some, paying for therapy actually adds insult to injury. On more than one occasoin, I have heard clients say, "My parents screwed me up, let *them* pay for it!" In many families, money and love are intertwined.

This is especially true in families where one or both parents are too preoccupied to spend time with their children and give them money and gifts instead of attention. For these children, money becomes a powerful symbol of love, personal value, and self-esteem. The attempt to avoid paying for therapy may be a way to manipulate the therapist into providing the love and affection the client lacks.

Therapists are often as ambivalent about collecting fees as clients are in paying them. *We* may come from families with money conflicts or have other issues concerning money, love, and self-worth. I've heard many training therapists say, "I became a therapist to help people and I feel embarrassed getting paid for it." Add to this the fact that we may be unsure of our own worth, and collecting fees becomes a significant therapeutic challenge.

One of my first private practice clients had a very difficult time paying for therapy and I had an equally difficult time confronting him about the money he owed me. He would go months at a time without being able to pay, bounce checks, and assure me that things were just about to turn around. He wasn't interested in a fee reduction, telling me I was a wonderful therapist and should be paid accordingly. He wasn't interested in going to a clinic with a sliding fee because he felt it was "beneath him." Not only was I embarrassed about bringing it up, but I also soaked up his praise like a sponge, all the while allowing him to accumulate thousands of dollars in unpaid bills. Years after he stopped coming to therapy, I received a notice that he had declared bankruptcy and that the law had forgiven his debt to me.

In retrospect, and with many more years of experience, I can clearly see how I failed this client in not discussing issues around money. His large bills, grandiose plans of future success, and praise for me were all aspects of his narcissistic defenses. I swallowed his fantasies hook, line, and sinker. If I could do it over again, I would address the issue of fees from the start. We would probably have discussed his injured self-esteem and how he needed to look realistically at the treatment he could afford.

This discussion about fees could have provided a window to the deeper issues with which he was struggling. Instead, my own embarrassment and lack of experience led to the reestablishment of a relationship that did my client little good. Ironically, he paid exactly what his therapy was worth. Over the years I have learned to be less fearful about discussing money during fee setting and reminding clients at the end of sessions about paying before they leave. When clients tell me that they can't afford my fee, I may suggest that they bring in their tax return so we can discuss the issue of finances in more detail. After an initial surprise on their part, they often tell me about their finances in great detail. It seems to be a relief just to talk openly about such a taboo subject.

It is probably a good idea to have a standard policy of how long you will go without payment to help you address these issues in a timely manner. Perhaps a one-month limit on missed payments should be standard before you postpone or discontinue treatment. Of course, every situation is different and you can't abandon a client of limited means. A standard policy should apply especially to clients whom you feel are not paying due to issues of resistance that need to be confronted in order for successful treatment to occur.

Making Interpretations

Successful therapy is a "safe emergency" that depends on a continual balance of support and challenge. With one hand we hold onto our clients to give encouragement and strength; with the other, we sword fight with their defenses. The use of interpretations is one of our most valuable sword-fighting techniques.

When we hear people telling a half-truth or fooling themselves with false beliefs in general conversation, we smile, utter some cliches, and move on to the next topic. Interpretations, like silence, are a violation of social norms. You are guaranteed to stop a conversation dead in its tracks when you say, "You are just saying that because you can't handle the truth." The vast majority of social conversation functions on the implicit agreement that "I won't call you on your act if you don't call me on mine."

Making an interpretation is essentially calling someone on their act. Interpretations attempt to make the unconscious

conscious by challenging beliefs, naming resistance and defenses and adding new and challenging information to the client's conscious awareness. Because interpretations are difficult to assimilate, their dosage and timing are important. Consider these strategies when making interpretations:

- Don't make an interpretation the first time it occurs to you. Be patient, think it over, listen thoughtfully, and gather evidence.
- When making an interpretation, try to incorporate the client's own words, images, and metaphors.
- Be prepared for your interpretation to be rejected.
- Don't push a rejected interpretation.
- If your interpretation *is* rejected, put it in the back of your mind for later.
- If your understanding is right, there will soon be another opportunity to offer it again in another way.
- Don't forget that you may be wrong.

After an interpretation hits home, remember that your client will need time to assimilate it. Accurate interpretations are a challenge to psychic equilibrium and those that are not deflected by the client's defenses result in a release of emotions. When an interpretation makes a defense conscious, it is rendered less effective, and the feelings it was inhibiting are released. That is why when an interpretation hits home, you may notice your client's facial expression changing; he or she may appear to become deflated, sad, or tearful. When this occurs, talk less and shift to a supportive stance. These moments are key in maintaining the vital balance of challenge and support.

Stan came to therapy because he was concerned about his

relationship with his children. Neither his adult son nor his daughter would speak to him and he couldn't understand why. All he knew was that they told him that he made them feel badly about themselves and they no longer wanted him to "contaminate" their lives with his negativity. "Can you imagine that!" shouted Stan. "I bring them into the world, raise them, put them through college, and now they don't want any part of me!" He repeated this refrain for the first 2 months of treatment and rarely let me interrupt him.

Near the beginning of the third month, Stan came in and opened the session by sarcastically asking me how I earned my money. "I do all the talking, you just sit there, and then I give you a check. What a racket you have here." My reflexive response was to tell him that he never gave me a chance to get a word in edgewise, but I soon realized that his transference had become activated. He was now doing to me what he probably did to his children. Here was my chance to earn my check. "I'm glad you mentioned this, Stan," I said. "You've talked a great deal about your wife and children but I wanted to know about your childhood and your relationship with your parents."

Stan had grown up as one of five children in lower Manhattan with two parents who worked in the garment business. Life was tough, money was tight, and his parents spent most of their time taking care of the family business. Unfortunately, his parents took their tough business personas home and dealt with their children as if they were competitors. Stan toughened himself up, became a successful businessman, and carried on the tradition of family communication through blunt confrontations and attacking the weaknesses of others. He was able to remember how he longed for tenderness from his parents despite the many times he was shamed by them for failing at sports or getting a B on an exam. He told me of how he and his brothers had subsequently experienced difficulties in relationships, substance abuse, anxiety, and depression.

To test his ability to tolerate an interpretation, I suggested that his asking me at the beginning of the session how I earn my money was how his parents would confront him. He smiled faintly and said, "That was nothing." I then tentatively asked if he sometimes treated his children the way he treated me and perhaps the way his parents treated him. From the expression on Stan's face, I could tell that he was making the connection between his childhood and his children's experience of him. The realization that he had recreated his own childhood pain within his children was devastating. He quietly stared at the floor, his eyes welling up with tears. No more interpretations were warranted and it was time to be as supportive as possible.

We later talked of how, with the best of intentions, parents often pass the pain from their own childhood to their children. I assured him that by working together, we could change some of his behaviors and attempt to heal some of the damage in his relationship with his children and grandchildren. Thus, in this brief period of time, I had shifted from a stance of challenge to one of compassionate support. If I had reacted to Stan's initial confrontation with defensiveness, he would have labeled me an incompetent wimp. By understanding and interpreting the transference, I was able to link his children's emotional experience to his own. This created the possibility for Stan to replace a critical style with an empathic one with people he cared about.

Remember, defenses gain strength when attacked. The key is to absorb the transference, not get defensive, and interpret what you consider to be the emotional process taking place. Care and patience always trump strength and aggression. Also, be patient with yourself; you will gradually improve at making interpretations. Simply said, it is an extremely complex and delicate process that requires lots of practice.

CHAPTER NINE

In the Eye of
the Storm
The Therapist's Challenge

If you're going through hell, keep going!
—WINSTON CHURCHILL

THE EYE OF A STORM is a place of calm at the center of chaos and confusion. You become the eye of your client's storm through the calm and centeredness you carry within yourself. Becoming centered is difficult enough; *staying* centered in the face of someone else's storm is a real challenge. As Buddhists say, it is easy to be enlightened on a mountaintop but difficult in the world of people.

In earlier chapters, I discussed some of the challenges of getting and staying centered. The next important aspect of the inner experience of being a therapist is what I call *shuttling*. Shuttling is the ongoing exploration of yourself and your client by means of a shifting attention across different aspects of your experience. It is the movement of your awareness inside of yourself, over to your client, and back again. Within yourself, during the session, you are shuttling your attention between your own thoughts and feelings as you monitor your fantasies, bodily states, and intuitions. I think of this in terms of shuttling *up* into my head and *down* into my body. Within the client-therapist relationship, you shuttle your focus among your own perspective, what you imagine your client's perspective to be, and your best guess about what is going on in his or her internal world. Imagine this type of shuttling as going from yourself across to your client and back again.

Think of shuttling as an open exploration, moving your conscious awareness through your body and over to your client, all the while being on the alert for potentially valuable information. The information comes in many forms: ideas, visual images, physical sensations, emotions, or memories. Whatever you notice can then become subject to conscious consideration. It is vital to explore with an open mind and not become attached to what you think you may have found. Sometimes what you find may mean something and other times it may not.

Just the other day, I sat across from a young man who was telling me how well everything was going for him. Jack described his promotion at work, the women he had been dating, and how he had finally reached his long-term fitness goals. As I listened, smiling at his good fortune, I became aware of wanting to cry. My first thought was that I was having an allergic reaction, but the feelings in my face and eyes seemed connected to genuine sadness.

As Jack talked the feelings persisted so I decided to share them with him. I told him, "I know you're telling me about all of these truly wonderful things, and I'm happy for you. But I want to share that as I listen to you, I'm feeling sad. I don't know whether these are my feelings or your feelings, but I wanted to share them with you to see what you thought." As I spoke, he grew quiet and I noticed that his eyes became a bit moist. After a while, he told me he felt sad and empty inside, and that he suddenly realized that he was distracting himself by focusing on his accomplishments. By naming the feelings I experienced in my own body, I was able to help Jack feel his feelings and recognize a defense against them. This served as a transition point from defensiveness to vulnerability, and he began to tell me about his emotional struggles.

Shuttling is necessary because of two fundamental weaknesses in our experience of ourselves and others. The first is that sensations, emotions, and bodily states are capable of disconnecting (dissociating) from conscious awareness. The second is that we influence one another in many unconscious ways. These processes make moment-to-moment understanding of what is happening in intimate relationships extremely complex. Successful therapy demands that we use our heads and hearts, minds and bodies, and knowledge and instincts because they can all be important sources of information.

Shuttling, like all other exploratory behavior, ceases in the face of anxiety. Think of an animal at the first moment it senses a predator; it freezes, assesses the source of danger, and prepares to fight or flee. When therapy becomes emotionally charged, the therapist is at risk of losing the ability to shuttle. Shuttling requires centeredness, calm, and flexibility.

Shuttling Between Yourself and Your Client

Our attraction to social information is reflected in the popularity of gossip, biographies, and celebrity magazines. Primates have elaborate brain networks dedicated to interpreting the actions and intentions of others through body language, facial expressions, and eye contact. Whereas evaluating others has a long evolutionary history and complex neuroanatomy, *self-awareness* has evolved in the more recent past. This may explain not only our tendency to discover ourselves in our experience of others but also why it is sometimes unclear where we end and others begin.

Many times while making an interpretation to a client, I am struck by how much it applies to me, as if I have tossed them a ball that turns out to be a boomerang. When this happens, I wonder, "Who am I thinking about, my client or myself? Do I see him, or am I seeing a projection of myself?" I may *never* be entirely sure. Given the way our brains process information, we can never know others unalloyed by our own inner worlds. Everyone we know is partly a reflection of ourselves.

Given the amount of projection involved in our experience of others, it makes sense that we may unconsciously use our clients to work toward solutions to our own problems. When these boomerang interpretations occur, you need to attend to the issues in your life that relate to your client's struggles. As your insight into your own process increases, go back and reevaluate your view of your client's issues. This back-and-forth process is necessary to counter our natural tendency to see ourselves in others.

Empathy is often confused with sympathy, compassion, and emotional resonance. Although these are all important aspects of intimate relationships, empathy is somewhat different. Empathy is a hypothesis or educated guess concerning your client's internal state. It is a method of observation that relies on your interpersonal sensitivities and skills, combined with your capacity to think about what you are feeling. You dip into another's experience as best you can using your emotions and imagination, then subject your experiences to conscious consideration in light of your knowledge and training.

I once supervised a graduate student named Michael whose mother had schizophrenia. He described to me how each day after his father went to work, his mother would gather up his toys and take them into her room, locking the door behind her. Michael would spend his days alone, his mother locked in her room. Before his father returned home, she would come out of her room and replace Michael's toys. Pretending they had spent the day together, she would tell her husband of the games and activities she and Michael had enjoyed. Michael spent the day in frightened isolation and the evenings in bewildered silence. He tried telling his father the truth but wasn't believed. As he described his early life to me, I imagined his pain, fear, and confusion. I had fantasies of breaking down the mother's door to retrieve his toys, and setting up cameras and tape recorders to provide his father with proof.

In entering into his experience, I became vulnerable to painful angry feelings and shared these with Michael. My strategies to "bust" his mother with cameras and tape recorders made him laugh, and then cry. He was surprised by my anger at his mother because he was only aware of his fear, pity, and loyalty. My physical and emotional response to his experiences generated the hypothesis that he might have angry feelings that he did not allow himself to feel.

Michael soon realized how helpless he felt in the face of his mother's abusive behavior. He also understood that he never thought of getting angry because he was so afraid of his mother's response to anything but compliance on his part. Sharing these experiences with me and allowing me to become involved in his inner world provided the grounds for our alliance. In Chapter 12, I'll come back to Michael and discuss how his childhood affected his work as a beginning therapist.

Shuttling Between Mind and Body

Human beings are complex social animals with subtle means of receiving and sending information to one another below the level of conscious awareness. We call the experience of this communication "gut feelings," "vibes," or "intuition." Although we are often unable to directly access these communications, they may affect our emotions, bodily sensations, thoughts, dreams, and fantasies. By shuttling down, we begin to access our inner world and use it as a potential source of information about our clients.

Shuttling down requires a shift in attention from thoughts to emotions and bodily states. When I shuttle down, I concentrate on my chest and stomach to try to become aware of any tension, fear, longing, sadness, or emptiness I may be feeling. Shuttling up to your conscious rational self allows you to then think through what is happening within yourself and your client, remind yourself of your case conceptualization and treatment plan, and make decisions as to how to think about what you are experiencing in your body.

Whether you are shuttling up or down, it should be an ongoing process that is carried out while you are attending to what your client is saying. Here are some clues about when to shuttle.

Shuttle Down:

- When you haven't for the last few minutes
- When you feel emotionally disconnected from your client or yourself
- When you feel consistently lost in or confused by your client's content
- When you find yourself distracted
- When you sense that your client is experiencing emotions that he or she is unable to express in words
- When your interpretations are being rejected

Shuttle Up:

- When you haven't for the last few minutes
- When you feel anxious, lost, or confused
- If you are feeling afraid or threatened
- In a crisis situation when you need to manage an emergency
- When you find that you have fantasies, memories, or feelings bubbling up within you

Some years ago, I did a classroom roleplay with a male student in his mid-forties. We played therapist and client to demonstrate some therapeutic techniques. As we spoke, I found that it was difficult to follow the logic of what he was saying. His sentences were grammatically correct but his overall communication lacked coherence. I just could not follow him. After checking in with myself to look for any obvious signs of countertransference, I shuttled down to see what I could find in my body. As I imagined shifting my consciousness down into my chest and stomach, I started to feel constrained, almost suffocated. Breathing was difficult and my body felt frozen in place. An image then came to mind; I was an old wooden barrel, held together by flat metal hoops. Although these hoops felt constricting, it seemed that without them, I would fall to pieces.

While my "client" continued to talk, I shuttled back up to my head to think about the image that my body had offered me. During a pause, I asked his permission to share the image of the barrel. As he listened, he slowly began to cry. When he was finally able to speak, he told us that his fiancee had been killed in a plane crash a month earlier. He said he had been walking around in a fog since the funeral, barely holding himself together. He was avoiding the reality of her death by keeping active and socializing as much as possible. At this point, I realized his words made no sense because their purpose was not to communicate but to distract us from his pain. He didn't want to think clearly about such a cruel and meaningless world. I suspect he needed me to put his feelings into words so he could begin to cope with them. In fact, he later told me that our work together in class was the beginning of his grieving process.

I have been able to gain insights such as this on many other occasions by remaining open to the feelings and images that come from shuttling down. Still, I'm never sure if they have anything to do with the client or are simply a reflection of my own issues. Even with the example above, the feeling of being a barrel could also be interpreted as my feeling trapped by someone who was trying to control me with words. I share these images with clients as products of my own imagination, and leave it to the client to accept, reject, modify, or ignore them. Some clients just roll their eyes and move on whereas others immediately relate to what I may share. It is important not to become attached to whatever you find and let it go if it doesn't serve the therapeutic process.

Learning From Distraction, Boredom, and Fatigue

In the midst of therapy, my mind can easily drift from my client. Sometimes I find myself thinking about buying a new car or what to cook for dinner. Other times my thoughts drift to people, places, or seemingly random memories. These thoughts may mean nothing. On the other hand, they may be a manifestation of countertransference and be completely about me. My feet may hurt, I may be tired, stressed out, or distracted by something outside of the therapy relationship. These random thoughts could be trying to tell me something important about my client or our relationship.

Then there are times when I find that I am not thinking about much of anything during a session. I "check out" when I don't want to take responsibility for the session and allow my client's content to carry our interactions without being actively engaged. It often means that I have colluded with the client's defenses by allowing his or her words to keep me at an emotional distance.

When you are feeling distracted, bored, or tired during a session, begin the process of shuttling in order to explore any manifestations of countertransference. Begin in your head and think through any reasons external to the therapy that might be causing you to feel like you do. Next, shuttle down into your body to find if you are angry, hurt, disappointed, or frustrated. If in the process of shuttling down you become aware of feeling anger and hurt, ask yourself whether your client has done anything that may have triggered these feelings. "Am I really bothered by the way she canceled the last two sessions or dismissed my last interpretation?" "Is my distraction a way of checking out on this client or is it a form of punishment for how his made me feel?"

Some clients are able to make us feel as emotionally disconnected as they are, either through mind-numbing detail or by excluding all emotion from their communication. Our reaction may be a collusive defense that allows the client to stay detached from his or her feelings while we remain detached from our own. I find whenever I'm fatigued in a session, the client is usually expressing very little affect. If I can snap out of my lethargy and somehow activate the client's emotions, I immediately wake up and feel alert and engaged.

A client's unconscious can lure us into an emotional resonance with his or her internal world. The power of such a potentially intense connection can have profound effects on our memory, orientation, and clinical judgment. The impact clients have on us as they lure us into their storm can provide us with vital information for the treatment process. To be involved enough to receive complex and primitive communications, while retaining sufficient objectivity and distance, is part of the delicate balancing act we perform as therapists.

On Being Tied to the Mast

Remember how Ulysses tied himself to the mast of his ship as it passed the island of the sirens? He had been warned that the sirens' call would be so alluring that there would be no resisting, and he would steer his ship into the rocks and be ruined. Being "tied to the mast" has become a metaphor for getting the help you need to resist overwhelming temptation. In psychotherapy, we depend on training, self-insight, and self-control to be our ropes in order to resist the call of unconscious manipulations by our clients.

Clients come to therapy with well-practiced relationship patterns and will tempt you to play a central role in their drama. If they have been a victim, they may engage in behavior that seems designed to get you to abuse them; if they have been dependent, they will try to get you to take charge. If a client's identity is based on a history of rejection, the client will do what it takes to get you to reject him or her. Depending on your theoretical perspective, these repetitive interpersonal dynamics could be called *attachment schema, repetition compulsion,* or *implicit memories.*

Your challenge as a therapist is to join clients through understanding, attunement, and empathy, while side-stepping their drama. You witness, understand, and interpret their drama without colluding in its reenactment. The more the client's drama resonates with your own (and the less insight you have about your own unconscious processes), the more vulnerable you are to participating in a regressive interactive reenactment of your mutual childhoods.

The reenactment of old relationships can be understood as a form of resistance that keeps the client from taking the risk of having a new kind of relationship. The brain has learned it can survive old relationship patterns, however painful, and so repeats them. The primitive survival networks deep within our brains prefer the devil they know to the devil they don't.

The Seduction of Words

On occasion, clients become so overwhelmed by life that they fall into a chasm of isolation and become mute. Reaching these clients requires that we climb down into that chasm with them and help them to regain their voice. More often, though, the client brings us a *torrent* of words, story after story, embedded with personal and family myths, interpretations, and rationalizations. These clients explain how they see themselves, what went wrong, and who is to blame for their unhappiness. The stories contain contradictions, misinformation, distortions, and some downright lies. Not only are these clients attached to their stories, but their identity is largely created and maintained *by* the stories.

A common error for new therapists is to mistake a barrage of words for openness and vulnerability. The relief in having a client talk and save us from awkward silences can make us forget to consider how the content may serve a defensive function. You never know during your first sessions if the client's content is a genuine attempt to be understood or an elaborate smoke screen designed to obfuscate and confuse. Being *superficially deep* may allow the client to remain *deeply superficial.*

With the best of intentions, beginning therapists try to follow every word their clients say. We struggle to follow their logic and make sense of their stories. My experience of clients with a barrage of words is like dodging a wild horse that is galloping around the room in frantic circles. Trying to engage in a discussion in these situations is a bit like grabbing the horse's mane and being carried around in its mad dash. Needless to say, the ability to stay centered and guide therapy while clinging to words for dear life is nearly impossible.

Some people learn during childhood that it is dangerous to think logically and to see the world clearly. This is especially true for people who grew up with abuse, addiction, and neglect. Their scattered attention and use of language have been shaped to keep them from gaining a clear experience of reality. The disorientation and disorganization that results from this defensive strategy is part of the storm they bring to therapy. In these situations, your confusion, numbness, or "checking out" may be important clues about your clients. This may be how *they* feel, or they may need you be numb or confused in order for them to feel safe.

One clue that you have grabbed the wild horse of words is that—no matter how hard you try—you can't understand what your client is talking about. If you are a basically intelligent person, and what your client is saying doesn't trigger any significant countertransference reaction, you should be able to follow his or her logic. As a therapist, you have to have enough confidence to think, "If I can't understand something after an honest effort, there is a good chance that the words are hiding crucial information."

Use your confusion as a possible clue to a client's defenses and try some of the following:

- Ask the client to repeat what he or she has just told you.
- Ask the client to help you to understand.
- Shuttle down to check out what you're feeling.
- Ask yourself what might the client *not* want to say or feel.
- Check for possible countertransference.
- Get supervision.

I have told clients and students many times, "I just can't follow your logic," to which they often reply, "You're not the first person to say that." Only through a relationship with a compassionate other will they will be able to examine their illogic, explore the reasons for it, and begin to monitor and organize their thought processes.

Talking Less and Saying More

A steady stream of words can serve as a manic defense, distracting us from painful or anxiety-provoking feelings. Like a small child covering his ears and humming when his parents are telling him to go to bed, we can drown out uncomfortable realities with our own words. In situations where clients are hiding behind a barrage of words, it is important to help them to *talk less* and *say more*. It is first necessary that we not employ the same defense, otherwise the sessions will turn into a "talkfest." Try to give your client three messages: this defense was once very important, but now it is hurting you, and it may no longer be necessary.

If you are able to deal with silence and the feelings that emerge, there are a number of ways to help your clients explore what is behind their stream of words. Try some of these approaches:

- Model comfort with silence from the first session by remaining relaxed during pauses in the dialogue.
- Inquire about feelings, thoughts, fantasies, and memories that may emerge during silence.
- Discuss the role of words and silence in the client's family of origin.
- Ask the client to sit in silence and state single "feeling" words (sad, mad, bad, glad, etc.) about every 10 seconds, this will help the client shift from rapid-fire narratives to basic feelings.
- Interpret the possible defensive nature of the client's talk by saying something like: "Sometimes talking can distract us from difficult feelings" or "Long and complicated sto-

ries can sometimes hide simple truths. Can you think of
any of your own simple truths?"

Interpreting silence can help deepen therapeutic interactions. When words are a defense, focusing on content may
further the client's unconscious agenda of avoiding deeper
feelings and more significant issues. Overall, it is important to
move therapy in the direction of process instead of content
interpretations. To focus on process means to ask about and
explore the emotional meaning behind what is discussed by
clients. Process interpretations are much more difficult to
make than content interpretations, but they are significantly
more helpful to the deepening of the therapeutic relationship
and the client's progress.

By making process interpretations, you call clients on their
act and possibly "out" their defenses. This may make your
client sad, anxious, or even angry. This is where your self-
knowledge and maturity come into play. If you are not prepared for your client to become angry or displeased with you,
you may be tempted to grab the mane of the content horse
and go for the ride. Unless you rein in that horse, you will sac-
rifice the potential for positive change. Therapy will then be
about the client's words, not about the emotions, defenses,
and coping strategies that cause him or her difficulties.

Still, you may find it necessary—as a strategic decision—to
follow the content for a period of time to make your client feel
more comfortable. This is sometimes wise in early sessions,
during periods of intense stress in the client's life, or after
some hard therapeutic work. The risk is giving your client the
impression that therapy is about the content of his or her
words. Stay aware of this possibility and, as always, think in

terms of balancing confrontation with support, and challenge with nurturing care.

Paying Attention to Dreams

Another form of shuttling that occurs outside of the therapy room is to pay attention to our dreams and what they reveal about our clients and ourselves. Freud called dreams the "royal road to the unconscious," speculating that in sleep our defenses become less effective, allowing access to usually hidden aspects of experience. Dreams can also make us aware of countertransference issues and subtle communication from our clients.

My dreams have helped me on a number of occasions with clients. In one instance, I had a dream about waking up one morning to find that I was not alone. Although I wasn't alarmed to find someone next to me, I had no idea who it was. After a while, I realized she was a client I had been seeing for over 2 years. She looked at me, said good morning, rolled over, and went back to sleep. Although being with her felt natural, it was also clear that something was amiss. Not only did I realize it was wrong to be in bed with a client, I was also surprised at having no memory of how it happened. The more I thought about where I was, the more tense I became. I was soon awakened by my escalating anxiety and relieved to find that it was just a dream.

As my relief gradually wore off, my curiosity grew. What did this dream mean? Did I have romantic feelings for this client? Try as I might, I could find no such feelings, thoughts, or fantasies. The next step was to consider whether my dream was an expression of signals I was receiving from my client. Although she was a single woman and around my age, I was not aware of her expressing any sort of attraction to me. But was this true? Was I missing something? Without telling her about the dream, I decided to explore her feelings about me.

During the next session, I encouraged a general discussion of our relationship, asking her to tell me any thoughts, feelings, or fantasies she may have had about me as a person or a man. Sure enough, we were soon having a discussion about her romantic feelings toward me, unexplored emotions related to her father, and questions concerning her sexual orientation. These interactions revitalized therapy and we moved to a deeper level of work.

This is a good example of how a dream can be used as information for the therapeutic process. My countertransference was primarily in the area of not picking up on her feelings for me sooner. As a child and adolescent, I was quite overweight and had a great deal of insecurity about my appearance. I learned not to pay attention to other's reactions to me because when I did, they were usually negative. Because of the continued presence of this early defensive strategy, I tend to miss signs of people being attracted to me. This client may have been giving me clues all along that I blocked out, misinterpreted, or simply overlooked. With subsequent clients, I have tried harder to force myself to examine this aspect of the relationship. Each of us has a mosaic of information-processing biases based on our learning histories. This is one of my many blind spots. One of the regular stops on our shuttle always needs to be to a consideration of countertransference.

CHAPTER TEN

Turning Weaknesses Into Strengths

The truth, that truth that lies buried beneath the roles, the costumes, the scenarios of life, is never forgotten.
—SANDOR MORAI

HAVE YOU EVER NOTICED that the people who know the least about something seem to have the strongest opinions? Those who never travel hold the strongest beliefs about other countries, those who never interact with people of other races have the strongest prejudices, and those who express the narrowest range of emotions speak with the most "expertise" about how to deal with feelings.

Because the brain's job is to predict and control outcomes, we become anxious in the face of ambiguity and confusion. The anxiety of ignorance drives us to manufacture certainty out of thin air. Although this is easy to see in the confabulations of clients with brain injuries and psychosis, it is more difficult to spot in so-called normal folks like ourselves. How do we work against this basic human drive and maintain an open mind? We begin through expanded awareness, openness, and the understanding that our perceptions are vulnerable to all sorts of biases.

There is much to learn before we can gain an appreciation of what we do not know. That's why it is essential that you remain as open as possible with your supervisor. We learn to trust our knowledge and judgments based on how well they match those whom we trust to teach us. Supervisors need all the information you can give them in order to do the best possible job.

Taking Sides and Neutrality

For primates such as ourselves, there is safety in numbers; we instinctively (and reflexively) take sides. We form groups, armies, and religions, expanding our self-identity to include sports teams, countries, and ideologies. This same instinct, in a therapeutic context, leads us to ally with our clients against others in their lives. Although building such an alliance has positive aspects, it also has pitfalls. Taking sides tends to polarize our perceptions in our client's favor. It also encourages the assumption that we are more like our clients than we actually are.

The information we receive from clients represents their interpretation of events and embodies their defenses, biases, and distortions. To the extent that we are privy to only one side of the story, clients are in control of what we know about them. What they tell us is biased, even when they are being totally honest. Acceptance of their perspective is only helpful to the degree to which it is accurate. Keep an open mind about what you are told and consider each client's defenses and emotional agenda when struggling to decipher what may actually be happening. I often find it helpful to have clients bring in family and friends to provide me with alternative views of a client's strengths, weaknesses, problems, and promise.

Besides our bias towards alliance, we are also vulnerable to breaking neutrality based on countertransference. Young therapists are prone to siding with children against parents whereas older therapists may tend to side with the parents. A male therapist may tend to side with a male client against his wife, especially if the therapist is having difficulties in his own marriage. A romantic or erotic countertransference may cause the therapist to be jealous of a client's relationship. He may then side with the client against her mate in an unconscious attempt to undermine the relationship. In each of these examples it is easy to see the potential damage that can be caused when therapeutic neutrality is violated.

That being said, if you are going to err, err on the side of allying with your client. Alliance and advocacy support the formation of a strong initial bond, and there will be time, once the therapeutic bond has been solidified, to test the accuracy of a client's perceptions. The challenge is greater in couples and family therapy, where you have to maintain a neutral stance while simultaneously building an alliance with clients in conflict with one another. In therapeutic situations, pay attention to your biases and explore their potential roots in countertransference. Violations of neutrality, especially when strong and sustained, inevitably spell trouble.

A therapist siding with a wife who describes an unreasonable husband may tend to downplay, or miss completely, the personality traits that make being in relationship with her client so difficult. An authoritarian father may terrify a therapist as much as the rest of the family. This can lead a therapist to take sides with the father due to her own fear and lack of power in her family. We are human before we are therapists and have all of the feelings and needs of our clients. Paying attention to our reactions and possible biases provides information about our own unconscious psychological struggles. This information can then become part of our awareness of how our own biases may affect our work with our clients.

Reality Drift

Our moment-to-moment experience is the product of a dynamic tension between our conscious awareness and our unconscious emotional self. Although we try to stay grounded in the present and mindful of our training, we naturally tend to drift in the direction of our early childhood experiences. If we are taught by our professors to maintain boundaries in therapy, but were trained by our family to violate them, we are always at risk of drifting in the direction of that initial training. Remember, we live simultaneously in the present *and* in the past, because past experiences have organized our brains, which, in turn, organize our experience.

I supervised a young man named Keith who complained of a high level of anxiety during sessions and of feeling like "the invisible therapist." The focus of our work was to help him speak more openly with his clients and take the risks involved in making confrontations and interpretations. Keith shared his family history with me to help me understand the background of his present difficulties.

His father worked as a geologist in the oil industry, and Keith's family spent his early years traveling around the Middle East. He described his mother as emotionally unstable with rapidly shifting bouts of anger and depression. His father was able to soothe her only after considerable patience, affection, and effort. Keith, unfortunately, lacked his father's skills. In the long hours while Keith's father was at work, the smallest thing could trigger his mother's anger, and Keith was incapable of calming her down.

Keith shared one particular memory that gave me a sense of the physical and emotional danger he experienced during his early years. Between the ages of 5 and 7, he lived with his family in a region where the midday temperature commonly reached 120 degrees. One day, a minor infraction of his mother's rules caused her to fly into a rage. As her anger peaked, she tossed Keith out the front door and locked it behind him.

He pounded in vain on the heavy wooden door, trying to get her to let him in. His bare feet burned on the stone walkway and he screamed in pain. She ignored him. The only shade he could find was under a neighbor's car, so Keith flattened himself and slid beneath it. He remained there for hours, baking in the heat and struggling to breathe. Finally, his mother called him inside. Other incidents like this were repeated throughout his childhood.

It was no mystery why Keith had difficulty sustaining intimate relationships. He was so afraid of triggering anyone's anger that the idea of disagreeing with other people filled him with fear. As a therapist he found that he had to force himself to make the most neutral statement, and even then, he would brace himself for the retaliation he was sure would follow. The thought of confronting a client or making an interpretation made his heart race. Keith was simultaneously an adult therapist and a frightened child alone with an unstable mother. Like Keith, we all have multiple, simultaneous realities superimposed one upon another in our day-to-day experience.

The work that Keith did in supervision and personal psychotherapy resulted in slow but steady progress. He gradually disconnected the memories of his early victimization from his work as a therapist and learned that he could tolerate and survive his clients' negative emotions. It was clear, however, that, under stress, he could sense himself drifting back to terror. He gauged his level of stress by examining just how present he would allow himself to be.

Years after our supervision ended, Keith told me that he had become much better at being emotionally present and having the courage to say things that made others uncomfortable. He did say that his new abilities had created difficulties in his relationship with his mother. Now that he was less terrified of her reactions, he was more open about sharing his feelings with her. Keith had discovered that part of his unconscious motivation to become a therapist had been to understand his mother's behavior so he might be more like his dad and overcome his terror of other people.

It is completely understandable that we use our personal experience as a standard against which to measure the thoughts, feelings, and behaviors of others. It is impossible not to have our own experience influence our work. If we have taken a drug successfully, used certain parenting skills with our children, or had a number of clients who have done well with a particular form of treatment, we will no doubt be biased in the directions of these things. Therefore, on a regular basis, we have to stop and ask ourselves:

- Why or on whose authority am I guiding my client in one direction or another?
- Where is my knowledge coming from?
- What is my sense of certainty based on?
- How much solid information do I have?
- Have I forgotten to keep an open mind?
- Have I drifted away from my training?
- Have I drifted back to some of my early defenses?
- Do these ideas really apply to this particular client?

Our clients are not alternative versions of ourselves, they are separate people with different minds, hearts, and histories. Although personal biases are impossible to avoid, we must continually attempt to be aware of them and factor them into our understanding of our clients. I am wary of therapists who begin sentences with the statement "Based on my clinical experience. . . ." What I hear is: "Here is my opinion wrapped in my professional status." Someone's perspective of his or her clinical experience is only as good as the person's knowledge, skills, and freedom from bias. Be cautious about presenting your personal opinions as professional judgment.

False certainty comes in many disguises. It can come in the form of feelings of pity, impatience, disgust, or annoyance. Being patronizing, condescending, bored, or indifferent may all reflect a sense of certainty and a disinterest in the essential process of your client's discovery.

Knowing Your Stimulus Value

Knowing your stimulus value is just a fancy way of saying, "Be aware of the reactions people have to you." We all embody a gender, race, age, personality, and set of physical character-istics in unique combinations. We have accents, rates of speech, ways we carry ourselves, styles of dress, beliefs, and attitudes. Any and all of these evoke varying reactions in different clients. Some reactions are based on societal values, others on the personality and past experiences of the client. Most are a mixture of the two.

A client once told me that she was unable to continue work-ing with her previous therapist because her therapist had gained a great deal of weight during her treatment. She expressed the belief that the therapist could not possibly pro-vide her with good treatment because she was so out of con-trol of her own impulses. Her weight gain had a stimulus value for my client steeped in cultural prejudice and personal history. It turned out that this woman had struggled with her own weight when she was young and was still terrified about gaining it back. Being in the same room with the therapist filled her with a fear of losing control herself.

Because we tend to avoid, deny, or distort things that we find emotionally troubling, awareness of our stimulus value can turn a potential weakness into a strength. The therapist who kept gaining weight never discussed it with the client who switched to my practice, despite the fact that she knew it was an important personal issue for her. Had she been able to discuss it with her and share her own concerns and diffi-culties, she might have opened the door for the client to work through some of her own fears and concerns. The more we avoid our struggles, the more they impair our therapeutic skills and abilities.

It is often difficult for a supervisor to bring attention to training therapists' stimulus values without making them defensive. Naming problematic issues triggers shame and activates defenses in supervision, just as it does in psychotherapy. I supervised a young gay man who was strikingly handsome and wore a diamond stud in his ear and tooled cowboy boots. To my eyes, Eric looked every bit a fashion model. He was very bright and our discussions of his clients were quite sophisticated; Eric demonstrated a great deal of knowledge and insight for his level of training.

After a couple of supervision sessions, I realized that Eric never mentioned any transference or countertransference issues. Although he was aware of them on a theoretical level, he never applied them to his own work. The disparity between his ability to discuss other aspects of the case and his inability to discuss transference or countertransference made me suspect that he didn't factor himself as a person into the therapeutic relationship.

When I asked Eric what he thought his clients' reactions to his physical appearance might be, Eric became defensive. He immediately wanted to know what was wrong with the way he looked. I had struck a nerve: Eric had a difficult time looking at himself and his effect on others without its triggering shame or self-criticism. He eyed me with suspicion and I knew this was our next area of work.

In the context of this discussion, I found out a little about Eric's history. Although he had suspected he was gay from an early age, his highly religious, small-town environment led him to keep it secret from everyone, including himself. He simultaneously carried a great deal of shame and covert excitement about his sexuality. All of his sexual encounters were made in secret with others who were also in "deep cover." When his parents found out, they sent him away to a deprogramming center to "fix" his homosexuality. His "treatment" included humiliation, isolation, and physical abuse in an attempt to get Eric to conform to "God's will."

Eric longed to escape to a place where he could discover himself and be with others who understood and accepted him. He left home the day he turned 18, first to college, and then to graduate school, where he was able to explore his sexuality in increasingly open ways. His clothing, earring, and style were part of this exploration. I met him at a time when these external changes were far ahead of his internal transformation.

In contrast to his attention-grabbing appearance, his childhood had taught him that being noticed was dangerous and shameful. The disconnection between this inner belief and outer presentation is a clear example of the mind's ability to dissociate aspects of experience that are obvious even to the most naive observer. Eric's brain had been shaped to keep these realities separated and unintegrated. He had spent his childhood presenting a false persona to those around him and he felt as if bringing attention to his appearance would "out" him. He wasn't aware that his current appearance was outing him and that he was going to have to become accustomed to people's knowing he was gay.

Before we could move forward with supervision, Eric needed to know I respected him and his sexual orientation, that I did not believe it was an illness, and that it would not be used against him when it came time for me to evaluate his work. "I think your goal of being openly gay is right for you," I told him. "But you have to remember that people are going to react to it and you need to be aware of and open to their reactions. You are going to have to cope with clients who feel everything from curiosity and sexual attraction to criticism and disgust."

Eric's past experience made his sexuality a matter of right or wrong. For some of his clients, it would be the same. Clients who have prejudices and fear related to homosexuality would likely reject him. He would also evoke sexual transference from both male and female clients based on his appearance. He might not be taken seriously by some older, more conservative clients, whereas those struggling to discover and express themselves in a similar way to Eric might find him the perfect screen onto which to project their erotic fantasies. The therapist's job is to be aware of what judgments, attitudes, and feelings he or she might evoke, and include this awareness in working with clients. If the first order of business is awareness, the second is understanding and growth.

Confidentiality

Although most therapists appreciate the importance of confidentiality, few of us speak about how difficult it can be to maintain. Humans are very social creatures who stay connected through a constant exchange of facts, stories, and free associations. Content analysis of everyday conversations reveals that the vast majority concern nonvital information. Most of what we say for the purpose of connecting us with others is a variation of "What's up?" Therefore, whatever comes to mind that is interesting, juicy, or emotionally stimulating rushes to escape our lips.

Early in my career, I supervised a student for over a year. I sat in the observation room each week watching him through a one-way mirror as he worked with his client. Although the client and I had never met face-to-face, I spent a year watching her and learning about her life. One day, I was walking down the street and saw her coming the other way. Momentarily, I forgot the context in which I knew her. Just as I gave her a big smile of recognition and began to say "Hi!" I remembered *how* I knew her. I recovered from my momentary lapse and apologized, saying that I thought she was someone else. As she walked away, I was impressed with the challenge of monitoring work-related experiences in such a way as to keep breaches of confidentiality to a minimum.

Keeping secrets is difficult. Secrets feel special because we know something that someone else doesn't, but they also create an internal pressure to tell and to see the other's reaction. Confidentiality is secret keeping in a professional relationship. If you have trouble keeping secrets, you are probably at greater risk for violating confidentiality. I always encourage students to be strict with themselves about confidentiality so as to heighten their awareness of its importance and difficulty. Students' first reaction to my rigid standards is to bargain with me. The questions usually start out with the phrase "Is it okay to tell when I'm talking to . . ." followed by all sorts of people like "my spouse, my family, people who don't know my client, people from out of town and so on."

Another question I have heard many times goes like this: "How could it possibly get back to the client if I'm vacationing in Italy and I tell someone I meet about a case I'm seeing back home?" Although I admit that it is unlikely, strange things do happen. I'm impressed by how often people I meet on vacation know other people I know at home. Of course, there are always the horror stories of talking about a client to someone over dinner and having the client or someone he or she knows overhear you from the next booth. You owe it to your clients to maintain their confidentiality as much as humanly possible.

Confidentiality is far more important to the therapeutic process than anything you might gain by violating it. Confidentiality isn't just an ethical principle and legal requirement, it is an inherent aspect of your clinical training. If you find you have the urge to gossip about a client, explore your countertransference. Be aware of the things you feel an urge to share and the feelings behind them; you may uncover reactions you have to them of which you were unaware. A therapist chooses to be in the background and, for some therapists, this is difficult to tolerate. Some therapists live *through* their clients and much of their social conversation is made up of talking about them. Although they may protect their identity, it is clear that their clients are their social world or a connection to things they lack.

Some talk about their clients to aggrandize themselves. Imagine having a movie star or famous athlete in your practice. It isn't wrong to feel important by association; it isn't even wrong to feel the urge to tell others or to want to impress your friends. The problem begins when these human qualities actually interfere with your ability to maintain confidentiality. If you need to talk to someone about a client you are seeing, even if it is just to relieve the pressure of knowing them, talk to your supervisor or pick another therapist who can provide peer supervision. Enlist the therapist's help in seeing if there are any ways that your need to tell someone may be interfering with your judgment or the therapeutic process.

Turning our tendency to gossip into the strength of strict confidentiality is difficult but vitally important. It provides

our clients with the freedom to share shameful and dangerous information with us while providing us the opportunity
to maintain appropriate boundaries between the therapeutic
relationship and all others. You will find that maintaining confidentiality will make you more certain of your own maturity
and professionalism, while deepening your sense of personal
integrity.

PART THREE

Getting to Know Yourself

CHAPTER ELEVEN

Uncovering Countertransference

All sorrows can be borne if we put them in
a story or tell a story about them.
—ISAK DINESEN

COUNTERTRANSFERENCE MANIFESTS in psychotherapy when our learning histories, coping strategies, and defenses interfere with our objectivity and adherence to the treatment contract. In other words, our needs lead us to make our clients' therapy about ourselves. Countertransference doesn't announce its arrival, it sneaks in and becomes part of the therapeutic relationship. Although it is certainly preferable to catch it before it manifests, we have to expect that we will most often discover countertransference after it has arrived.

A number of years ago, I supervised a doctoral student named Jamie who was working with Beth, a depressed woman in her early thirties. He described her as "slowed" in her movements, continually sighing during the session, and expressing many sad thoughts. Jamie was alarmed by Beth's depression and felt she needed immediate and active interventions to get her "up and moving." He gave me the tape of their fourth session so I could give him additional feedback during our next supervision session.

It was an interesting session and I was impressed with Jamie's level of activity and use of humor. He was extremely quick-witted and found humor in nearly everything, stopping just short of telling knock-knock jokes. I enjoyed Jamie's humor and level of energy but was unable to get a sense of Beth. He had her speaking to empty chairs, roleplaying, and engaging in expressive exercises like a new-age guru. Only toward the end of the session did I realize how little attention either Jamie or I had paid to the client. I rewound the tape and listened again.

On second listening I heard Beth make multiple attempts to get Jamie's attention. She wanted to discuss her relationship with her boyfriend, her problems at school, and an upcoming visit by her mother. Her attempts were either ignored or given passing attention as Jamie continued to direct the focus of the session. I could hear the pressure in Jamie's voice and his need to keep the interaction positive and upbeat. As I listened to the tape, it became clear that the session was driven by Jamie's anxiety. I didn't know Jamie well, so I had no idea why he was having such a strong reaction.

I started off the next supervision by complimenting him on his enthusiasm and knowledge of various intervention strategies. As we listened to the tape together, I shared my impressions about his anxiety and possible countertransference reaction to Beth's depression. As I described my impressions Jamie became visibly sad. Listening to the tape was very painful for him; he requested time to work through his feelings before we discussed it further. He took the tape and left.

Jamie came to our next supervision session having listened to the tape a few times and spoken with his therapist. Fortunately for Jamie, he had the courage and intelligence to weave together his inner experiences with his clinical training. Over the next few weeks, Jamie shared with me that his mother was chronically depressed. He had vivid memories from childhood of his mother's inability to get out of bed for days at a time. Fearing she was dead, Jamie would sit silently at her bedside, staring at her chest to make sure she was still breathing. Jamie shuddered as he recounted these memories.

Jamie had suffered with his own bouts of depression. As a young boy, he had become good at elevating his mom's and his own mood with humor or excitement about some activity they could do together. He became a class clown; decades later, he was known at his university as the life of the party. For the first time Jamie connected the manifestation of his countertransference to the underlying emotional issue. Jamie realized that his humor and activity in the session were tied to his need to stave off his depression and his frightening memories of childhood.

Jamie now understood that sitting across from his client, a depressed woman about his mother's age when he was young, unconsciously activated fear and sadness from his past. This was his countertransference issue. His twin childhood missions of cheering up his mom and distracting himself from his own depression had become activated. Jamie could not see the client in the context of her present reality and instead was transported into his own past. He was once again a frightened boy hoping his mother was still alive. The impact of his countertransference on Beth's therapy was obvious.

Manifestations and Underlying Issues

Our first clues to the existence of countertransference come when we happen to notice thoughts, feelings, and behaviors that are out of alignment with a neutral stance or sound therapeutic strategies. In Jamie's case, the humor, lack of silence, all of the activities, and his lack of attention to Beth's feelings and needs were countertransference *manifestations*. At first, neither of us knew what the countertransference *issue* was, but we knew something was going on.

Other countertransference manifestations may be that you look forward to a session or, conversely, dread its arrival. You may pound away with interpretation after interpretation or, as a friend of mine used to do, "forget" to unlock the waiting room door when a particular client was scheduled to arrive. Countertransference-based behaviors are out of line with your training, intentions, and the best interests of your clients. Discovering the countertransference issues underlying these manifestations is the next and more difficult challenge.

The unconscious motivation for countertransference most often comes from early negative experiences related to acceptance, abandonment, trauma, or shame. In Jamie's case, the overwhelming fear related to his mother's depression activated a variety of old strategies to cope with the memories triggered by his client's depression. A general rule of thumb is that countertransference reactions are triggered by anxiety linked to our formative history and deeper emotions.

For primates such as ourselves, early survival depends on two basic elements: the integrity of our bodies and our attachment to and acceptance by our parents and caretakers. For a young child, both physical and emotional abandonment are experienced as life threatening. Being shamed is experienced much like abandonment and has a profound impact on our attachment patterns, brain development, and self-identity. Children who experience physical trauma, abandonment, and excessive shaming early in life have a greater likelihood of both psychological and physical difficulties later on. It turns out that what doesn't kill us often makes us weaker.

For nearly two decades, my psychotherapy classes have been filled with students who have suffered (and are still suffering) from early negative experiences. This is why the focus of my classes has shifted from an emphasis on the techniques of therapy to an exploration of the *therapist's* inner world. I found that when techniques are taught before countertransference issues are identified and addressed, the techniques are used to satisfy the therapist's unconscious emotional needs.

Although many training therapists have not experienced severe early trauma, most everyone has had experiences during childhood that made them afraid, ashamed, and concerned about whether they were acceptable, loveable, and worthwhile. As normal human beings, we learn to live with our self-doubts and manage our anxiety without becoming debilitated. The unique environment of psychotherapy, with its strong regressive and emotional elements, makes it powerfully evocative of feelings and memories we may otherwise be able to repress. Even the most psychologically healthy therapists are subject to countertransference reactions. Being a good-enough therapist cannot mean the absence of countertransference—it can only mean having the skills to identify and work with it when it arises.

An Exercise in Uncovering Countertransference

The following exercise is the best I know of to learn to identify countertransference issues. It takes time, work, a good supervisor, emotional honesty, and courage. If you put hard work and heart into this assignment I guarantee that you will be repaid for your efforts by becoming a better therapist.

Step One: Start by picking a challenging client, one with whom you seem stuck, experience strong feelings, or have a suspicion that you may be having countertransference. Don't forget to tell your supervisor about this assignment, what you plan to do, and involve him or her in the process as much as possible. Share as much of this material with your supervisor as you can and definitely bring it to your personal therapy.

Step Two: Once you have chosen a client, *begin to jot down your personal thoughts and feelings in a countertransference journal.* Pay special attention to distractions, dreams, or fantasies you might be having and just free-associate to any aspect of your experience related to the client. Begin with a focus on your client and gradually shift to a focus on yourself in relation to your client. In other words, pay less attention to your client's problems as you shift to a focus on your experience.

Step Three: Tape record two sessions a few weeks apart. Make sure that you discuss this with your client beforehand and assure him or her of confidentiality. Tell the client it is part of your training and that only you and your supervisor will have access to the tapes and any transcriptions. You may even offer the client the tapes and transcriptions after you are through with them. If they do not wish to be tape recorded select another client. Most clients are flattered to be the focus of your attention and happy that you take your training (and their welfare) so seriously. Don't forget to keep a running journal of your experiences before, during, and after the recorded sessions.

Step Four: Review your tapes and journal entries to see if you can identify any manifestations of countertransference. Think about your experiences before, during, and after the sessions as well as what you actually did and did not do during them. Focus on the tone of your voice and the symbolic value of what was said. Following are some specific thoughts, feelings, and behaviors that may contain manifestations of countertransference:

- Feelings before and after the session
- Silence—too much or too little
- Fear of confrontation or upsetting your client
- Making no interpretations or too many interpretations
- Saying too much or too little
- Arguing with your client
- Missing or avoiding the client's emotions
- Going off on tangents
- Personal disclosure or telling stories
- Missing important details
- Distractions and daydreams

Although none of these are necessarily manifestations of countertransference, they are often fertile ground in which to discover clues of underlying countertransference issues.

Step Five: Transcribe the tapes verbatim from start to finish. Include pauses, "hmms," and other sounds. This may be tedious but is very important. Think of it as a form of meditation. As you listen to the tapes in the detail required to transcribe them, the content becomes familiar, and you will focus more on the *emotional process* between you and your client and, then, within yourself.

Look for feelings and memories that emerge during the transcription process and note them in your journal. Following these associations, connect your experience in the sessions with your life outside of therapy and your personal past.

Step Six: Find two or three underlying countertransference issues to analyze. Countertransference issues will be the underlying emotional struggles that result in the manifestations you observe in your sessions. For example, Keith's manifestation was his silence in therapy and his underlying issue was fear of punishment and abandonment. Jamie's humor and level of activity were manifestations, and his underlying countertransference issue was warding off his fear of his mother's depression and what it meant about his own safety and worth as a person.

Use whatever evidence you have about yourself to discover your countertransference issues. It may be helpful to include feedback you have received from friends, colleagues, relatives, employers, therapists, and supervisors over the years. Was there any feedback that was especially upsetting? Remember that you are *looking through a glass darkly;* there are large portions of your mind defending your conscious awareness from what you are seeking to discover. Don't be surprised to find that you procrastinate in doing this task or employ avoidance strategies such as cleaning, eating, shopping, or playing computer games far into the night.

Often you will only glimpse your own truth out of the corner of your eye, in the form of vague impressions that may, at first, elude you. Pay attention to your dreams, fantasies, and random thoughts; they may hold clues for you. Remember, the brain is incapable of random responses, so keep questioning and stay curious. Sometimes a cigar is just a cigar; sometimes it represents something else.

"Things Were Just Perfect"

Autumn looked perplexed. As I described this countertransference assignment, her confusion continued to deepen. At the end of class, everyone left but Autumn. She sat in her seat and stared at me with a bewildered expression. I went over to her and sat down. She seemed both scared and concerned. "I've had the perfect life, a great childhood, and wonderful parents. How am I going to do this assignment? I don't have countertransference issues and I'm afraid I'm going to fail this class."

There is usually someone in every class who begins the semester this way. They are always bright, attractive, well organized, and good students: the perfect package. Their clothes are right and they possess all the social graces, though they do seem to care a little too much about their grades. Adjectives they prefer consist of "really good," "really nice," "really great," and "awesome." Any critical analysis is avoided like the plague.

Autumn worked diligently in the face of her confusion, frustration, and concern. I encouraged her to imagine how it would be if she weren't perfect, if she hadn't lived up to her parents' expectations, if she hadn't been a cute cuddly child, or if (God forbid) she got a B on her paper. All of these ideas seemed inconceivable to her. Yet, in listening to and transcribing her tapes, she found that not only did she not challenge her client, but she also utilized a litany of excuses to *avoid* confrontation. "It's just an assignment, I'm not a real therapist, I didn't want to upset him, he has enough to deal with in his life already." No matter what happened during her sessions, she would never say anything that carried the slightest risk of making her client uncomfortable. She justified her rationalizations in a way that prevented her from finding any countertransference. Autumn had unknowingly mislabeled important countertransference manifestations as strategies.

Finally, close to the end of the semester, the pieces began to fall into place. Autumn began to remember experiences of not being perfect. There were times, during her early childhood, when she disappointed her parents and they turned their attention to her brother. To earn it back, she learned to do the things her brother did and ignore what was important to her. She realized that she didn't want to upset her client by confronting, interpreting, or asking for clarification because, at an emotional level, she was trying to figure out whom her client wanted her to be. Autumn's focus was "How can I be the person he will like?" rather than how she could be the therapist he might *need.* She had uncovered an important countertransference issue.

Autumn didn't have the perfect childhood. What she did have were selective memories that were interpreted to be perfect. Her mother needed to be the perfect mother; if Autumn was the perfect child, her mother fulfilled her own dreams. And if Autumn remembered her childhood as perfect, her mother loved and accepted her because her memories supported her mother's needs. As long as she was perfect, her mother and father had been perfect parents. She was even named Autumn because it was her parents' favorite time of the year.

Autumn needed to discover more fully who she was in order to be good-enough for herself and her clients. The assignment reminded her that she had left a part of herself behind. To become a good-enough therapist, Autumn had to let go of being the perfect daughter in order to access to *all* of her thoughts and emotions. The assignment began a process of self-discovery that was both difficult and rewarding for her. It was painful for her to realize that she wasn't perfect but a relief to find out that she didn't have to be in order to be a good therapist.

Society teaches us to hide our weaknesses and play to our strengths in countless ways. From inflating our resumes to avoiding horizontal stripes, we try to make a good presentation and sell a positive image. In our training as therapists we have to work against this strong cultural bias. We need to gain conscious awareness of our weaknesses and share them with others in order to change them into strengths.

CHAPTER TWELVE

The Making of a Caretaker

Where we are born is the worst kind of crap shoot.

—ANN PATCHETT

NO ONE IS A BORN THERAPIST. We are sculpted to be caretakers in early relationships and later resculpted during professional training. Each therapist is a unique blend of early experiences and clinical training, one unconscious, the other conscious, one during childhood, the other as an adult. The focus on countertransference in this book is an acknowledgement of the power of early childhood training and its covert influence on conscious behavior throughout life.

As I mentioned earlier, most groups of training therapists contain students who adamantly insist that they had perfect childhoods and that any countertransference that does exist is superficial and easily rectified. Provided with a way of detecting and examining countertransference, they discover the childhoods they *actually* had versus the combination of parental and personal defenses that have been woven into family myths.

It is not a random choice to become a therapist. Innate dispositions combine with environmental and parental influences to determine which children grow into caretakers. The choice of the caretaking role and how it is carried out depends on our attachment patterns, history of trauma and loss, family dynamics, and the challenges we faced while growing up. The motivation to help others comes from the combined needs to regulate others and heal ourselves.

The Vulnerable Healer

Although the vulnerability of healers has long been recognized, it needs to be rediscovered by each generation. Drug and alcohol abuse, depression, sexual and financial exploitation of clients, and suicide are risks therapists share with nurses, physicians, and clergy. Professional caretakers are simply ordinary people given extraordinary trust, responsibility, and power.

The power of the therapist combined with the privacy of the therapeutic relationship makes clients vulnerable to all kinds of exploitation. A therapist who feels empty, unloved, or powerless may find a client's loving attention in a private and confidential environment impossible to resist. I know a number of therapists who spent many years and huge amounts of money to become educated, licensed, and build a practice, only to lose it all in a moment of bad judgment.

Addictions are common in the childhood families of caretakers. Alcoholic parents are unpredictable in their physical and emotional availability and often need their children to nurture them. They lack the ability to provide the stable emotional environment their children need to feel the world is a safe place. In turn, children of addicted parents often lack sufficient safety and nurturance, predisposing them to turn their attention from their own development to the needs of frightened and frightening parents.

Hypersensitivity to the feelings and needs of another makes one well-suited to being a successful child of an addicted parent. Additionally, early boundary violations and role reversals make violating therapeutic boundaries feel entirely natural despite all of our training. Parenting our parents make us, as therapists, vulnerable to having our unconscious needs met by our clients.

Having parents who tend toward obsessive-compulsive defenses are also extremely difficult for children. People with these defenses attempt to manage their anxiety with rigid and repetitive behaviors like cleaning, deodorizing, and organizing. These defenses conflict with the reality of normal children who are often smelly, sticky, disorganized, and unpredictable. Children of these families experience their parents' discomfort, anxiety, and disgust with most everything they do. The identity of these children becomes a reflection of their parents' rejection and constant correction. In this way, the parents' anxiety is converted into the child's shameful self-image.

Sadly, most of my students had one or both parents incapable of being "good-enough" at parenting, and had to learn to survive in dysfunctional family systems. Their brains were shaped by their early experiences, creating difficulties with self-identity, self-esteem, and the ways they behaved in subsequent relationships, both personal and professional. These adaptations are reflected in countertransference manifestations and issues we discover during training.

The Therapist's Childhood in the Consulting Room

Being too anxious to speak during sessions is a common countertransference manifestation in beginning therapists. Michael, the young man whose schizophrenic mother left him alone all day, struggled with this problem. I asked him to imagine saying to his client the things he was holding back and be aware of any thoughts, memories, or feelings that might bubble up. After a short time, Michael said, "I'm frightened. I can imagine my client yelling at me, telling me I'm stupid, and storming out of the room." I told him to stay with this image. Michael's face slowly grew fearful and then melted into sadness. He hung his head and sighed while I waited for him to speak.

"It feels like when I was a kid. I was alone all day. It feels painful, like a pain in my chest. The days seemed to last forever. I remember taking a brick from the walkway in the garden. I drew a face on one side of it and wrapped it in a dish towel. I would sit for hours holding my brick 'doll,' rocking back and forth, talking to him, and telling him I'd always be there to take care of him. Before my mother would begin with her afternoon routine, I would tell my doll to go to sleep until tomorrow, and put him face down in the garden.

"I was so afraid my entire childhood of what my mother would do next. I thought that even the few words I said to her each day were dangerous. When I'm doing therapy, I always want my clients to stay calm. When I think of saying something or making an interpretation, all I feel is fear. What will happen if I make them angry? I sit and stare at my clients like I sat and stared at my mother."

There are many people in the consulting room besides the client and yourself. Clients brings their families of origin and many of the people in their present life. Some of these people are referred to consciously whereas others are embedded in a client's self-image, character, and the way he or she attaches to you. You bring in your own cast of characters embedded in your personality, therapeutic work, and countertransference. They are present in your relationship abilities, your choice and use of therapeutic theory and techniques, and your emotional attunement and misattunement. The consulting room is a crowded place.

Pathological Caretaking

Pathological caretaking is a specific manifestation of a disturbance of self we refer to as *narcissism*. Narcissism is characterized by a two-sided self: one reflecting an inflated sense of self-importance, the other emptiness and despair. This formation of the self results from a child looking to the parents for love and attunement only to find the problems and needs of the parents. The child, lacking the help he or she needs to engage in self-discovery, compensates by caring for the parents under a real or imagined threat of abandonment. The bright and sensitive child learns to attune to and regulate the parents' emotions. The child will appear mature beyond his or her years, instinctively regulate the emotional experience of others, and adapt, chameleonlike, to different individuals and social situations. The inner experience of these children comes to reflect the needs of others.

The other side of narcissism reflects those aspects of the

child's emotional world that have found no mirroring. The true self, or the part that is unique to the individual, is neglected, underdeveloped, and waiting to be properly parented. This inner core of abandonment and shame is hidden beneath the inflated sense of self-importance generated by the ability to regulate others. A pathological caretaker may be a perfect child, an "A" student, or loyal friend on the outside, but an empty, sad, and lost child on the inside. Autumn's perfection, discussed in the last chapter, was an expression of her parents' needs and their adaptation to their own childhoods. Autumn's self was a family construction that did not include her feelings, needs, and desires.

The child's attachment schema becomes dedicated to attuning to the moods and needs of the parent and, then, to others. The child grows into self-awareness not just with the emotions of others experienced as its own, but also with a compulsion to regulate the emotions of others. Taking care of others serves as a substitute for self-soothing and inner emotional organization. For pathological caretakers, to feel is to feel bad. The result is that being alone is difficult and being with others requires a lot of work. A one-sided, or even abusive relationship may be less frightening than solitude and the feelings that might follow.

Caretakers make difficult clients because they learned early that when they are in distress, help is not forthcoming. At the core of their attachment relationships is the belief that others can be a source of responsibility, but not nurturance. As clients, pathological caretakers present as depressed and exhausted by their inability to keep up with the needs of others and the defenses they employ in order to stay one step ahead of their feelings. At the same time, as clients, they will try to turn the table on their therapists and attempt to take care of them.

Some indications that you may be a pathological caretaker include:

- Having to keep busy all of the time
- Finding it easy to stand up for others but impossible to advocate for yourself
- Finding it difficult to refuse the demands of others
- Experiencing other peoples' needs as your responsibilities
- Not being able to take help from others
- Having friends that require much *of* you but are unable to provide *for* you
- Finding socializing and relationships to be exhausting or avoiding them altogether
- Believing that "if you want something done right, you have to do it yourself"

The Gifted Child

The central importance of parental relationships in shaping the social brain is described in a series of elegantly written and deceptively simple books by Alice Miller. Her therapeutic work with what she called "gifted children" targeted adults who were raised by parents whose own emotional needs overshadowed their parenting abilities. Taking a stand against her analytic colleagues, Miller saw her role as one of an advocate for the child within her adult clients. Reaching back through the years to reconnect with long-forgotten childhood experience, Miller interpreted much of her clients' adult behavior as adaptations to the needs of their parents.

In her role as an advocate, she saw therapy as a process

wherein clients are assisted to unearthing their history, not from the point of view of the adult, but from the perspective of the child they once were. For Miller, gifted children are exquisitely sensitive to the cues of parents and have the ability to mold themselves to their parents' messages. These are the children who come to be called "codependent" and make up the bulk of service professions as doctors, nurses, social workers, and therapists.

Although the gifted children described by Miller may look quite functional, they often feel empty and devoid of vitality. Because their vitality and true self are not acceptable, they are inhibited and banished from awareness. This disconnection from the true self creates a vulnerability, not only to personality disturbances, but to the unconscious transmission of this same dynamic to the next generation. Parents who have not been adequately parented look to their children for the nurturance and care they were unable to receive years before. Miller (1981, p. 35) stated, "What these mothers had once failed to find in their own mothers they were able to find in their children, someone at their disposal who can be used as an echo, who can be controlled, is completely centered on them, will never desert them, and offers full attention and admiration." This same dynamic can be brought into therapy by the therapist.

The child's first reality is the parents' unconscious. Children's instinct to bond with their parents drives them to attach regardless of the terms and conditions. When the child looks into the mother's eyes and finds no reflection except the mother's needs, the child will mold him- or herself (if able) to meet these needs. The gifted child doesn't rebel, which becomes the heart of the problem. Unable to construct the story of their own lives, gifted children search for others who need nurturance. Miller felt that the child always needs an advocate because he or she is completely helpless in childhood to resist the coercion of the parents' unconscious. Because it is implanted in early unconscious memory, it is never experienced as anything other than the self.

Although clients do not have conscious memories of early relationships with their parents, Miller posited that these learning experiences are recorded in how they think of and treat themselves (self-image and self-protective behaviors). The strictness and negativity of how clients talk about themselves (superego) betrays their parents' negative attitudes toward them years before. These implicit emotional and behavioral memories, in the form of attitudes, anxieties, and self-statements, contribute to the continued repression of real emotions and the conscious awareness of one's own needs.

Caretaking and compulsive perfectionism also reflect the ongoing attempt to compensate for this deep inner sense of being unworthy of being loved for oneself. In line with this adaptation, psychotherapists often come out of childhood with strong conscious and unconscious needs to:

- Be perfect
- Be liked
- Avoid conflict
- Not have negative emotions
- Protect others from negative feelings
- Have few needs and no strong opinions

These tendencies are expressed in the therapeutic relationship as:

- Feeling total responsibility for the client's improvement
- Difficulties coping with silence
- Needing to be liked or be a friend to the client
- Siding with the client against others in his or her life
- Inability to tolerate the client's affect
- Keeping interactions at an intellectual level
- Giving advice

Shame-Based Experience and Behavior

Although a career as a psychotherapist provides us with the opportunity to parlay our caretaking defenses into a profession, an examination of countertransference almost always leads back to core issues of acceptance and abandonment. For example, therapists often play the role in their families of "affect regulator." That is, they modulate emotion within and between different family members. They are often the diplomat, the confidante, the negotiator, or the good child that didn't require much parenting. We often have siblings who were troubled and troubling to our parents and we made the decision not to add to their burden by having needs of our own. These aren't simply familiar roles for future therapists, they are the currency of acceptance into the family and thus the method and manner of survival.

By being "perfect," children spare their parents the pain of acknowledging their child's (and, by extension, their own) shortcomings. By drawing as little attention to themselves as possible, children can avoid being shamed for their behavior and thus remain connected to rejecting parents. A family unable to deal with conflict or negative emotions will train a child not only to keep from dealing with his or her own feelings but also to become skilled in diverting the entire family from going in that direction.

These adaptations may keep emotions in check, but life remains messy. When a client becomes angry, afraid, or confused, a therapist may unconsciously take the role he or she had in childhood and apply the rules of his or her family to the therapy relationship. As we have seen, a therapist can regress into a frightened child or struggle with posttraumatic symptoms of his or her own with certain clients at vulnerable moments. Although there are no rules about what direction our countertransference reactions will leads us, they all distort our perceptions of our clients and our ability to develop appropriate therapeutic strategies.

Becoming a Therapist

A question asked by many students boils down to: "All this consciousness raising, all this pain and discomfort, where does it get me?" The short answer is: "*What you resist persists.*" As long as our unconscious contains emotional memories that drive us to think, say, and act based on the past, we live under the control of the past. Although we are never free from the influences of the past, we can work to minimize them through conscious exploration, insight, and attempting to act in more positive ways.

Once we discover that we've chosen to be a therapist partly for unconscious reasons, what do we do? How do we decide to be a therapist for the right reasons, or at least reasons that are in our own and our clients' best interests? Some students choose to change careers and report feeling liberated from a lifetime of caretaking; they want to build a life that includes *their* needs. Many say that they needed time to discover what they liked and what their own needs were, especially because they had spent their lives mirroring the likes and needs of others. They wanted to develop a sense of their own preferences.

On the other hand, many students move into careers as therapists with a deeper appreciation of their history and predilections and a growing ability to take care of themselves. The best clinical training is a journey of inner growth advancing us into careers that are best for us.

CHAPTER THIRTEEN

Building a Satisfying and Sane Career
Cautions and Encouragement

Doesn't listening to people's problems all
day drive you crazy?
—THE GENERAL PUBLIC

HOW DO THERAPISTS stay sane? How *do* we listen to problems all day and not explode from the accumulated
pain and confusion? There are many factors to consider in staying sane and building a satisfying career. Some very important
aspects include understanding your limits, taking care of your
own needs, and being aware of the impact of our clients' suffering on our psyches. It also requires that we be well-trained,
stay connected to supervisors and peers, and abide by the ethical and legal guidelines of our profession. Together, the following principles will go a long way toward creating a satisfying
career while protecting your well-being and quality of life.

Principle One: Know Your Limits and Select Your Clients

How many hours of therapy should we do each week? I've
learned that I am at my best up to about 17 hours a week, after

which I begin to become exhausted, irritable, and distracted. I certainly lack the stamina of therapists who claim to happily see 40 or 50 clients a week. Pay attention to how your level of energy, stamina, and mood are affected by your schedule. This will help you to learn about your client/hour comfort zone. Talk to practicing therapists to find out about their everyday lives and think hard about your personal needs as you consider a career path. Choose a career with your eyes wide open.

Another rule of thumb is to chose your clients well. I always tell my students to limit their practice, if it is at all possible, to one borderline client at a time. Borderline clients are extremely difficult and can take as much emotional energy as all of your other clients combined. Their hostility, rage, suicide attempts, and criticism all take a toll. Chronically depressed clients are also extremely difficult to work with because their sadness can sap our energy and tap into our own sadness. Client selection, just like your overall schedule, is something you will learn to adjust over time. Don't worry about looking spoiled because you need to be careful about your caseload: You have to survive over the long haul.

Principle Two: Engage in Consistent Self-Care

We have to care for ourselves while caring for others. Providing good therapy and self-care are interdependent. When we find that work is pushing us to the point of exhaustion or depression, we need to look closely to see if we have fallen into patterns of pathological caretaking and self-denial. Good therapy should be healing and energizing for both clients and therapists. In general, you need to feel that you and your clients are growing from the therapeutic process. If doing therapy always feels laborious, stressful, or even painful, something is wrong. Carefully examine the state of your mental health and your life with your own therapist.

I spent many years running at full speed with little thought of my own well-being. Some of the best advice I ever received was: "Life is a marathon, not a sprint." Like a marathon runner, I needed to learn to pace myself, conserve energy, and focus on the process instead of the goal. I had to examine and change my concept of work. Having been raised in a working-class family, I thought of work as something that makes you dirty and exhausted. It took me a long time to comprehend *emotional* exhaustion and realize that, even though I was clean and comfortable, I had put in a long, hard day.

Stay alert to personal signs of overwork and use them as reminders to engage in self-care. One sure sign that I am overworked is a persistent dull headache that will not quit. I have gotten better at connecting that feeling in my head to my schedule and making time to relax. I spend many weekends in the country, take regular vacations, and always carry a good novel in my briefcase. Just making sure you take lunch and exercise each day can make a big difference in your mental outlook. Other signs of overwork might be not engaging in enjoyable activities, isolating yourself from friends and family, and finding it difficult to stop from time to time in order to relax. Not coincidentally, these are also signs of depression.

Don't underestimate the toll psychotherapy can take on your heart and mind. Stay mindful of your own physical and emotional needs, especially when taking on new responsibilities. It is easy for healers to forget that we aren't just adjuncts to the lives of others but rather have our *own* lives to live, too.

Because therapy is so complex, it is often hard to find clear signs of success. I need to complete tasks to feel good, so I find it important to engage in projects that have clear goals and visible results. Working on the house, cooking, even writing a book, allows for a clear sense of completion that is rare in psychotherapy.

What do *you* need to feel good about yourself and your life? Take the time to find out and pursue your passions!

Principle Three: Keep Perspective

Be on guard for the long-term effects of caretaking. The constant practice of putting others' needs ahead of your own can lead to compassion fatigue and burnout. We can eventually forget about ourselves and become a mirror that depends on the reflection of our clients. Our bodies and minds resonate to the emotions of others as we experience their pain. Even if you were not shaped to be a caretaker as a child, spending too many hours outside of your own perspective can be dangerous. Maintaining perspective includes the ongoing awareness that you are a human being first and a therapist second, and, always, a separate person from your clients.

If you suspect that you may be losing perspective, ask yourself some of the following questions:

- What influence does being a therapist have on me?
- Am I living vicariously through my clients?
- Am I getting enough of what I need outside of the therapeutic milieu?
- Am I following my passions?
- Am I getting enough nurturance?

- Am I willing to accept the nurturance available to me?
- Am I doing what I want to be doing?

The early psychoanalysts were notorious for their egotism, intolerance of other perspectives, and romantic escapades with disciples and clients. We all need to try to keep our egos in check, our authority in perspective, and our feet on the ground. Living in the world of the unconscious can make navigating day-to-day life more than a little tricky. It helps to have people in your life—like the client who reminded me I was a "suppository of information"—who help to keep your feet on the ground.

Principle Four: Watch Out for Traumatic Contagion

As social animals our brains resonate with the experiences and emotions of those around us. This means that trauma is contagious. Go to a conference for therapists who specialize in the treatment of trauma and you will notice a sea of anxious and depressed faces. When I spent a large portion of my clinical hours working with traumatized clients, I began to feel haunted by images of abused children, battered wives, and scenes of combat. Our vulnerability to one another is an integral part of our biology, not a sign of weakness or lack of professionalism.

When we are in the presence of a traumatized person, our brains become activated in the same ways as when we are traumatized ourselves. Not only are we not immune to our clients' pain, but we also must develop close and caring relationships in order to treat them. All of our clients bring us their suffering and we, in turn, internalize and digest it—at a cost.

Late in life, Carl Jung moved to the shore of Lake Bollingen in Switzerland. He lived and worked in a small medieval castle not unlike the drawings in children's fantasy books. In front of the castle was a flag pole to which Jung's friends and neighbors paid close attention. At various times Jung would raise a flag to signal them to stay away, and they would wait until the flag was lowered before approaching the castle. When asked about the flag, Jung described his need to be alone with his thoughts and feelings after seeing certain clients. He felt that he needed time to process what he had heard and gradually integrate it or wash it from his being. Jung clearly understood and appreciated emotional and traumatic contagion and how difficult it is to be a therapist.

Principle Five: Know Your Laws and Ethics

Lectures on professional law and ethics usually include statements such as: "I don't want to scare you, but. . . ." or "Don't get paranoid, but. . . ." Personally, I think it is good to be scared about committing malpractice or breaking the law. Be scared enough to carefully study the laws and ethical codes. Be scared enough to protect each client's confidentiality and to remember that the regressive environment of therapy makes you vulnerable to unprofessional behavior. Most importantly, be scared enough to remember that being a therapist is a big responsibility that needs to be taken seriously every day.

I remember the first time a client handed me a check. I stared at *my* name on the check and realized that the buck now stopped with me. There was no longer a supervisor to hide behind. *That* was scary!

It is essential to know and abide by the ethical standards of our profession. Although some of the rules may seem overly rigid or unnecessary, they reflect the accumulated wisdom of those who have already confronted and worked through the problems that lie ahead. Keep in mind that legal and ethical codes protect therapists as well as clients. Clients with a history of sexual abuse will often be attractive and seductive. One of my clients terminated after I refused to engage in a romantic relationship with her. Another was having an affair with her couples' therapist while she was seeing me for individual treatment. We are vulnerable to these clients, especially when we are young, attractive, and needy. In retrospect, I am deeply thankful for the emphasis my training placed on scaring me enough to maintain the boundaries of the therapeutic relationship.

I have conducted sessions outside of my office just twice in 20 years. One time came after an earthquake made my building unsafe, and the other time came when we were evacuated because of a fire. In both situations, I did not feel that canceling the session was in the best interest of the client. Seeing clients in your home, a backyard office, or in other such places can be easily misinterpreted and difficult to defend if you find yourself in litigation. Bartering services such as exchanging therapy for car repairs or tax preparation is also not a good idea. Always have a clear therapeutic contract that informs both you and your client of your rights and responsibilities. Nontraditional ways of doing business, despite their occasional convenience, simply are not worth the risk.

Reich suggested that behind every positive transference lurks a negative transference. You may violate the therapeutic frame with good intention and even obtain good results during a phase of positive transference. If and when the transference shifts, all of your behaviors will be reinterpreted in light of a negative emotional state. Meeting in a park, which seemed like a good problem-solving strategy when the building was on fire, may, at some future point, be interpreted as seduction, a date, or worse. A therapy relationship gone wrong can look very much like a hostile divorce.

To protect yourself you need to adhere to accepted standards of practice and avoid interacting in unusual circumstances and nontraditional ways. Your professional board and insurance company can support you best if you have practiced within the standard of care of your community. This will often differ depending on the mores, values, and resources of your community. Make sure you have a good idea of what these standards are, especially if you move to a new area of the country. What may be acceptable in Burlington, Vermont, may violate the standards of Natchez, Mississippi.

What They Don't Teach You in School

Graduate schools are good at teaching a professional language and a set of skills and providing the contacts you will need to get started in your career. Schools can also be good places to make friends and build a support system that can sustain you after graduation. What schools are not particularly good at is helping you to get to know yourself, your career options, and how to foster a good match between the two.

All schools promote their particular agenda. Large state universities promote careers in research and teaching, professional schools sell dreams of lucrative private practices in exchange for high tuition, other training programs encourage a life of community service. All of these career paths can be meaningful and satisfying. But which one is right for you? The vast majority of us make career decisions based on too little information. We rely on brochures, television programs, or the suggestion of a friend. Like many things in life, we choose without knowing the implications of our decision.

As a beginning therapist, get to know people who are doing what you think you want to do, and then spend as much time with them as possible. Get guidance and advice from people who share your interests, personality, and energy level. Ask lots of questions about lifestyle, income, stress, schedule, bureaucratic demands, and vacation time. These are the nuts and bolts of a career, and more important to making the right decision than any abstract concepts or fantasies you may harbor.

If you are choosing a school, find out where the faculty received their degrees. Read the books and articles they have written to see what kinds of thinkers and researchers they are and if their interests match your own. I always advise students to attend school where they plan to live after graduation. During school you get the opportunity to make connections that will serve as your future support network. Other professionals may be inclined to help you in your training and in establishing professional connections. When you show up in a new town with a degree and a license, you're the competition.

Money is also an important consideration when choosing a graduate program. Figure out the total cost of the degree (including tuition and living expenses) and subtract the amount of money you will be able to earn while in school. Translate the remaining debt into the monthly payment you will have to cover after graduation (including interest), and then add this to the cost of living and compare this figure to your likely take-home salary. This calculation will give you some idea of whether it is a good idea to go for that expensive private school or find a more economical alternative. If you come out of school with the equivalent of a mortgage payment before you have a place to live, life may get difficult and your options very narrow. It is an excellent idea to have a session or two with a financial advisor who will not only have a good idea about the expenses you will run into, but will also have the tools to calculate cost of living increases and long-term interest costs on the money you need to borrow.

What Therapeutic Orientation Should You Choose?

The prevailing modes of psychotherapy—cognitive behavioral (CBT), family systems, psychodynamic, and humanistic—all have something to offer to the right therapist and the right client at the right time. My suggestion is to get solid training in at least two methods of psychotherapy and select the best available supervisors regardless of orientation. The intelligence, maturity, and wisdom of good supervisors are far more important than whether or not they prefer Gestalt to CBT.

Our choice of orientation is not random; we may chose an orientation because we are searching for answers in our lives or because it fits well with our personality and defenses. My interest in psychodynamic therapy was motivated by an attempt to understand myself, just as my fascination with systems therapy was driven by a desire to understand my own family.

Students uncomfortable with ambiguity often chose CBT because it is structured, programmed, and avoids mucking around in the unconscious. It is an excellent way to avoid or stay in control of your feelings. Students drawn to psychodynamic therapy run the risk of getting tangled up in their own unconscious. Perhaps the best approach is to pay attention to what you are attracted to and use it as an indication of potentially important information about your unconscious motivations. Apply the shuttling strategy to explore this choice within yourself and discuss it with your supervisors and therapist.

I first met Dana as a student in an abnormal psychology class. I remember her because of her reaction to any reference to Freud or the unconscious. At the first mention of a psychoanalytic concept, she would launch into a monologue about the absurdity of such a preposterous notion as the unconscious. She criticized Freud from feminist, Marxist, and behavioral positions, and simply on the grounds that Freud was a cocaine addict. She made many good points, but it was clear that her crusade against the unconscious was more personal than intellectual; she protested much too much. Dana made it clear that she would only do CBT and was uninterested in considering alternate forms of psychotherapy.

Two years later, Dana reappeared in a small seminar on psychological assessment. My first thought when I spotted her was that it was going to be a long semester. By the third week we were discussing the Thematic Apperception Test (TAT), which is comprised of a series of pictures presented with the instructions of making up a story about what is happening in the scene. Of course, the test rests on the assumption of the unconscious and the process of projection.

I asked Dana to tell a story about the first picture, one that depicted a boy and a violin. "It's obvious," she stated. "The boy is being forced to practice, he hates the violin, and will never learn how to play because he hates it so much." I asked Dana,

"Can we learn anything about you by your response?" "No!" she said. "It's obvious just from the picture, there is no projection." I then asked her, "Would it make a difference if you knew that this is a picture of Jascha Heifetz as a small boy?" "That's impossible," Dana stated as I pulled photographs of the young Heifetz from my file. In fact, the creators of the test used a drawing taken from a photograph of Heifetz. She was stunned and sat silently until the end of class.

Dana called me to set up a meeting before the next class. She came to my office asking for a reading list on projective testing and psychodynamic therapy. "When you showed me that photograph," she said, "it was so clear that I couldn't possibly be talking about Heifetz. Who else could it be but me? I must have an unconscious!" She happened to be an avid fan of classical music and specifically of the violin. I had accidently found a window through which Dana caught a glimpse of her unconscious mind. She was engaging in her first shuttling experiences, examining her own emotional reaction to the demands and expectations she had projected onto the young Heifetz.

Many therapists are biased against medication and think of pharmacology and psychotherapy as mutually exclusive. This couldn't be further from the truth. Medication can be a very useful adjunct to psychotherapy. I have worked with clients who resisted taking medication for years only to experience rapid progress after finally agreeing to a medication trial. Some clinicians are adamantly against drugs, almost as if they are on a crusade against them. My experience is that these people are motivated by emotion rather than knowledge. Perhaps there was drug or alcohol abuse in their families, or they are dedicated to new-age philosophies; maybe they just lack knowledge about the wide variety of modern medications. Either way, it is a disservice to your client to be ignorant of or prejudiced against medication. Take the time to educate yourself, and find a good pharmacologist with whom you can work.

When you have a hammer, everything can begin to look like a nail. For zealous devotees of a particular school of therapy, all clients look like they need to be treated with what the clinician believes to be the one true way. Therapeutic approaches are based on theoretical heuristics, ways of looking at reality and human experience. The one true test of any therapy is its usefulness for a particular client. Ultimately, the four major modes of therapy are all important; we need to consider the individual and the family, the conscious and the unconscious, cognitions and emotions. So why choose? Use them, integrate them into your treatment, and try to stay open to new treatment possibilities. Use everything that is potentially helpful to your clients. Also, recognize that you may meet clients who need something you can not offer; familiarize yourself with alternative resources in your community.

Where Should You Work?

Therapists work in many different settings. Besides private practice, we can work in hospitals, community mental health centers, schools, clinics, and industry. Not only can we treat clients, we can also supervise other therapists, perform case evaluations and case management, and carry out administrative duties. This wide range of options is one of the very desirable aspects of our field.

Private practice is attractive because it provides the most independence and control over one's schedule. A successful private practice requires self-organization, motivation, and an entrepreneurial spirit. It helps if you are a social person who likes to participate in organizations and talk about what you do. I have found that the best way to market my practice has been to give talks and provide people with information and resources. It is also good to foster a few specialty areas so that you can write articles and have a focus for your talks. These increase your exposure to other therapists and the general public.

Although private practice is a good choice for many reasons, there are also some shortcomings. It is a business, your clients become customers, and things like marketing, expenses, and sole responsibility for a caseload have to be considered. How do the following sound to you?

- Selling yourself and promoting your practice
- No paid vacation
- Difficulty in getting time off
- Paying for your own medical insurance, malpractice insurance, and retirement benefits
- Having to start from scratch if you move to another city

Consider all of these things carefully before deciding on a private practice.

Another risk of private practice is that you are God in a universe of your own creation. Like priests, movie stars, and kindergarten teachers, therapists can suffer from having too much power over too many people. The lack of balanced relationships in private practice can contribute to reality drift and make the therapist dependent on his or her clients for human contact. If you choose private practice, make sure you have colleagues you can tell anything to, while maintaining confidentiality. Talk honestly with them about clients, and continue to get accurate and compassionate peer supervision and feedback whenever possible. These kinds of relationships and honest feedback are essential wherever you practice.

If you are not business oriented, self-motivated, or want to be free to move from place to place, private practice may not be a good long-term plan. And although being able to charge $100 or more an hour sounds wonderful, keep in mind that after taxes and overhead (rent, phones, insurance, etc.) you are left with closer to $40. I often joke with my students that the key to an enjoyable private practice is to marry rich. This way you can choose your clients, select your hours, and live in luxury. If you are not so fortunate, it is even more important that you are careful in making career decisions.

Other popular choices are working in hospitals, clinics, or community agencies. The advantages include a steady flow of clients, a regular paycheck, benefits, and an institutional affiliation. Institutions offer a social structure, backup, and shared "on-call" coverage that is important if you are the type of person who likes to turn your phone off on weekends. It is also much easier to move from place to place and find another job than to start and build a practice. Bureaucracies have their own dangers: not enough control of your work, demands for conformity, mountains of paperwork, and the inherent limitations of systems.

Some therapists work much better in institutions despite these problems and limitations. They are mature enough to persevere in the face of institutional realities and red tape. Their therapeutic interests and the population of clients they wish to serve are most easily accessed through institutions, and they are not demoralized by the inevitable interpersonal and economic politics. The question is not whether a particular venue is better or worse than another, it is whether the venue is a good fit with you.

CHAPTER FOURTEEN

Walkin' the Walk

> The life of a gentle highwayman is hard to
> lead well, but it is lit up by the joy of spring
> and always by the greatness of the sky.
> —LANZA DEL VASTO

YOU MAY HAVE NOTICED that this book is not about what a brilliant therapist I am. As I look back over the pages, many are filled with my confusion, countertransference, and ignorance. I couldn't have written this book when I first began my career because it took years for me to realize that being a therapist has nothing to do with being perfect. I always intellectually knew that no one is perfect, but the emotional reality of my own imperfection was difficult to swallow.

An essential part of becoming a therapist is the journey to self-acceptance in the face of our own limitations. Accepting ourselves *with* our limitations is very different from self-acceptance *despite* them. Although the difference may sound purely semantic, it is deeply experiential—we have to accept our limitations so that we can learn to work with and around them. Genuine acceptance of the whole person is what good-enough parents feel for their children and good-enough therapists feel about their clients. Embracing our own limitations, not simply tolerating them, provides us with the self-caring required for emotional growth. When we finally make friends with ourselves, we don't have to be so fearful of making mistakes.

Unfortunately, most training programs focus almost exclusively on "what to do" not "how to be." It is assumed that the latter is being handled in other places when this is often not the case. Most students dedicate very little time to expanding their self-insight and awareness. Becoming a therapist is on a list of things to do, and personal discovery is a vague and distant concept. In line with this same attitude, therapy becomes something to do *to* not *with,* clients. This has been reinforced by training programs that keep students busy jumping through hundreds of hoops with little emphasis on inner experience. Therapy is taught as a body of information, set of techniques, and lexicon of psychological jargon to learn.

I prefer to think of therapy more as a state of mind than an activity or accomplishment. This is why, over years of teaching, I have shifted from instructing students about the techniques of psychotherapy to teaching methods of self-discovery. An essential part of this is sharing some of the struggles of my own self-discovery, shortcomings, and disappointments.

My teachers and supervisors were not particularly open about their internal experience and the challenges they encountered during training. Perhaps it didn't seem appropriate to burden a student with their personal issues or perhaps they felt it was a violation of professional boundaries. I suspect that my training experience would have been quite different if my mentors did share more of their personal experiences with me. I wish they would have. I know that it was very difficult for me to imagine getting to where they were from where I started. It would have helped if I knew they overcame obstacles that were as large as the ones I seemed to be facing.

Mindfulness

I believe the key to being a successful therapist is self-awareness. Because of this, I feel it is essential to find ways of bringing mindfulness and an expansion of your self-awareness into everyday life. In writing this book I chose to focus on what is traditionally a psychodynamic perspective, which is why I used such terms as resistance, projection, and countertransference. But psychotherapy is only one of many ways to expand self-awareness.

Meditation, yoga, and martial arts can be used in this way, as can wisdom philosophy, spending time in nature, or playing with children. I find I learn a great deal about myself when I travel to other counties or gaze through a telescope at the night sky. The therapist's inner journey can be explored and enhanced through many perspectives and disciplines that focus on understanding the mind and the workings of conscious experience.

I invite you to think of psychotherapy not simply as a profession but a calling, a lifestyle, and a vehicle of personal growth. Therapists are people looking for answers. Don't settle on only finding the answers for your clients; find your own along the way. Find your own truth, discover your own passions, and don't settle for less.

Therapists can easily feel like frauds when there is a wide chasm between what they preach to clients and how they live their own life. There is little risk of feeling like a fraud if you honestly live the life you encourage your clients to strive for. By this I don't mean that you have attained all of your goals, but rather that you are aware of your feelings and desires, achieve what you can, and accept what is unattainable.

The experience of personal failure is an essential part of development. It helps us to learn about ourselves and is especially important in highlighting the strengths of our character. In the same way, failure in relationships provides the opportunity to repair what has been ruptured and teach us that mistakes, anxiety, and fear can not only be survived but also transcended and serve as a foundation for a stronger relationship. These are the good mistakes I wrote of earlier—a central part of the growth of individual character and strong relationships. The repeated experience of rupture and repair is central to establishing secure attachments to clients, to others in your life, and to yourself.

Reunion

After all the cautions, warnings, and red flags, why would anyone still want to be a therapist? Truth is, despite all of the difficulties, risks, and challenges, being a therapist can be incredibly rich and meaningful. Although one of the most difficult professions to navigate intellectually and emotionally, it offers us the opportunity to help others while simultaneously discovering ourselves, stretching us to our full human potential.

When clients ask me why I make the investment in them, I respond by saying that I believe in them, enlightenment does happen, and that we all have potential for positive change. Psychotherapy is a profoundly optimistic endeavor, and our optimism is one of our most important contributions to the therapeutic relationship. Although I can remember many therapeutic failures, I can also remember an equal number of successes.

One such memory is of a session with an aging father and his adult daughter. I had seen Ken for a number of years to help him be more aware of his feelings and express them to those around him. He was winding up a long career as a corporate executive who had committed his life to building a successful business. Unfortunately, he applied business strategies to his family life and provided his wife and children with a CEO instead of a husband and father. When Ken mentioned to me one day that his daughter Kelly was home for a visit, I suggested he bring her in for our next session. Ken had described Kelly as bright, beautiful, and troubled. He feared he was to blame for her problems.

Sitting at opposite ends of the couch, Ken and Kelly leaned forward nervously, wondering what would happen next. Ken cleared his throat and Kelly's eyes widened. With a little encouragement, he began describing the feelings he had for Kelly that he had never expressed. He vividly described his memories of her as a newborn, a toddler, a little girl, and a rosy-cheeked cheerleader and expressed his pride in her at college graduation. He told Kelly how bright and beautiful she was and how he hoped that, now that he was retiring, they would spend more time together. Kelly cried as she listened to his words and was drawn to her father like a magnet. They were soon in each other's arms, and I noticed a tear in Ken's eye. I felt one in my own.

Helping people connect with one another fills me with warmth and gratitude. Bringing hope to people without hope creates a feeling within me of a deeper connection with the earth. Being a catalyst for victimized clients to become empowered helps me believe my life has meaning. These peak experiences may not happen every day, but they occur often enough to keep me going.

These are rich and satisfying rewards—there are none better—and I wish them all to you.

References &
Suggested
Readings

Basch, M. (1988). *Understanding psychotherapy: The science behind the art.* New York: Basic.

Bloom, B. (1997). *Planned short-term psychotherapy: A clinical handbook.* Boston: Allyn & Bacon.

Castaneda, C. (1972). *Journey to Ixtlan: The lessons of Don Juan.* New York: Pocket Books.

Coelho, P. (1987). *The pilgrimage.* New York: Harper Flamingo.

del Vasto, L. (1974). *Principles and precepts of the return to the obvious.* New York: Schocken.

Dinesen, I. (1992). *Out of Africa.* New York: Modern Library. (Originally published 1937)

Giovacchini, P. (1989). *Countertransference triumphs and catastrophes.* Northvale, NJ: Aronson.

Hammarskjold, D. (1964). *Markings.* New York: Knopf.

James, R., & Gilliland, B. (2003). *Theories and strategies in counseling and psychotherapy.* Boston: Allyn & Bacon.

Kaslow, F. (Ed.). (1984). *Psychotherapy with psychotherapists.* New York: Haworth.

Kidd, S. M. (2002). *The secret life of bees.* New York: Penguin.

Kingsolver, B. (1992). *Pigs in heaven.* New York: Harper Collins.

Kottler, J. (1989). *On being a therapist.* San Francisco: Jossey-Bass.

Langs, R. (1976). *The bipersonal field.* New York: Aronson.

Levy, D. (1997). *Tools of critical thinking: Metathoughts for psychology.* Boston: Allyn & Bacon.

Lucas, S. (1993). *Where to start and what to ask: An assessment handbook.* New York: Norton.

Marai, S. (2002). *Embers.* New York: Knopf.

Masterson, J. (1983). *Countertransference and psychotherapeutic technique: Teaching seminars on psychotherapy of the adult borderline.* New York: Bruner/Mazel.

McClure, F., & Teyber, E. (2003). *Casebook in child and adolescent treatment: Cultural and familial contexts.* Pacific Grove, CA: Brooks/Cole.

Miller, A. (1981). *Prisoners of childhood: The drama of the gifted child and the search for the true self.* New York: Basic.

Natterson, J. (1991). *Beyond countertransference: The therapist's subjectivity in the therapeutic process.* Northvale, NJ: Aronson.

Patchett, A. (1997). *The magician's assistant.* New York: Harcourt Brace.

Perlman, S. (1999). *The emotional survival of the therapist.* Northdale, NJ: Aronson.

Piper, M. (2003). *Letters to a young therapist.* New York: Basic.

Reich, W. (1972). *Character analysis.* New York: Farrar, Straus & Giroux.

Robertiello, R. C., & Schoenewolf, G. (1987). *101 common therapeutic blunders.* Northdale, NJ: Aronson.

Shiraev, E., & Levy, D. (2001). *Introduction to cross-cultural psychology: Critical thinking and contemporary applications.* Boston: Allyn & Bacon.

Slakter, E. (Ed.). (1987). *Countertransference: A comprehensive view of those reactions of the therapist to the patient that may help or hinder treatment.* Northvale, NJ: Aronson.

Thoreau, H. D. W. (1995). *Walden.* New York: Houghton Mifflin. (Originally published 1854)

Vimalakirti (1976). *The holy teachings of Vimalakirti: A Mahayana scripture.* R. Thurman, (Trans). University Park: The Pennsylvania State University Press.

Yalom, I. (2002). *The gift of therapy: An open letter to a new generation of therapists and their patients.* New York: Harper Collins.